GCSE
English
Foundation Level

Complete Revision
and Practice

Contents

Contents

Published by CGP

Editors:
Josephine Gibbons
Heather Gregson
Luke von Kotze
Rachael Powers
Rebecca Tate

Contributors:
Tony Flanagan
Margaret Giordmaine
Jill Lessiter
Ian Miles
Lynn Weston

With thanks to Jennifer Underwood and Paula Barnett for the proofreading,
and Laura Jakubowski for the copyright research.

ISBN: 978 1 84762 579 3

Website: www.cgpbooks.co.uk
Clipart source: CorelDRAW®
Printed by Elanders Ltd, Newcastle upon Tyne.

Based on the classic CGP style created by Richard Parsons.

What You Have To Do

GCSE English exams — they're on their way. But they're <u>not</u> as scary as you think.

What you **Have to Do** depends on **Which Route** you take

There are <u>two ways</u> to study English at GCSE nowadays. You can take either:

ENGLISH LANGUAGE

AND   OR   **ENGLISH**

ENGLISH LITERATURE   = 1 GCSE

= 2 GCSEs   (which is mainly English Language, but has a bit
of Literature thrown in for fun)

Your teacher should be able to tell you which route <u>you're</u> taking.

You'll be **Assessed** in two **Different Ways**

1) Controlled Assessment *You'll have to do a series of tasks chosen by your teacher.*

2) Exams

Your GCSE(s) will be split into different <u>units</u>. You'll do an exam or controlled assessment for each unit.

What you'll be doing for **GCSE English**

The Exam

- <u>Section A</u> — <u>questions</u> about unseen <u>non-fiction</u> texts.

- <u>Section B</u> — <u>writing non-fiction</u> texts.

If you're doing WJEC, this will be two separate exams.

If you're doing Edexcel, the breakdown between the exam(s) and controlled assessment will be different. Check with your teacher.

Controlled Assessment

- <u>Creative writing</u>.

- Writing about literary texts (one by <u>Shakespeare</u>, one from a <u>different culture</u> and one from the <u>English Literary Heritage</u>, i.e. an old book or poem).

- <u>Speaking and listening tasks</u>.

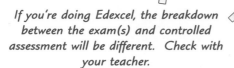

You need to know what kind of English you're studying...

Exams aren't much fun, but it's good to know what to <u>expect</u>. This page covers what you <u>need to know</u> if you're studying English. Turn the page for more on English Language and English Literature.

What You Have To Do

Another thrilling page — this one covers <u>English Language</u> and <u>English Literature</u>.

What you'll be doing for **GCSE English Language**

English Language is mainly about <u>your own writing</u>, <u>non-fiction texts</u> and <u>speaking and listening</u>.
If you're doing <u>Edexcel</u>, the way you're examined will be <u>different</u> from this so check with your teacher.

THE EXAM

- <u>Section A</u> — <u>questions</u> about unseen <u>non-fiction</u> texts.
- <u>Section B</u> — <u>writing non-fiction</u> texts.

This is exactly the same as the GCSE English exam(s).

CONTROLLED ASSESSMENT

- <u>Creative writing</u>.
- Read and write about an <u>extended text</u>.
- A study on <u>spoken language</u>.
- <u>Speaking and listening tasks</u>.

English Literature is a bit more **Complicated**

1) You'll have to study a <u>wide range</u> of texts — a mixture of <u>poetry</u>, <u>prose</u> and <u>drama</u>, including:

- a <u>Shakespeare play</u>
- <u>prose</u> from a <u>different culture</u>
- <u>contemporary</u> (modern) <u>drama</u> or <u>prose</u>
- <u>drama</u> or <u>prose</u> from the English, Irish or Welsh <u>literary heritage</u>

An anthology is a collection of poems for you to study.

- <u>poetry</u> (from an <u>anthology</u> or <u>chosen by your teacher</u>)

2) You'll have a combination of <u>exams</u> and <u>controlled assessments</u>.
3) You might have an <u>exam</u> question on an <u>unseen poem</u> — this will be a poem that you <u>haven't</u> come across before or studied in class.

Make sure you know what you're going to be studying...

I know, I know, it's a lot to take in. <u>Ask your teacher</u> if you're not sure whether you're doing Language and Literature or GCSE English. Then settle down with a cup of tea and <u>enjoy</u> the rest of this book.

Planning

You've got to make a <u>plan</u> for <u>every essay</u> you write. That's a plan <u>on paper</u> — not in your head.

Decide what to say *Before* you start *Writing*

Think about what you're going to write <u>before</u> you start — that way your ideas will have a clear structure.

> Good writing <u>makes a point</u>. It doesn't just ramble on about nothing.

In an exam, try to come up with <u>enough ideas</u> to keep you writing till your time's up.

Leave yourself about 5 minutes to check through your work though.

Stick your *Points* down on *Paper*

1) Before you start writing, spend about <u>5 minutes</u> jotting down a <u>plan</u> of the points you want to make.
2) Don't bother writing your plan in proper sentences.

> Q1 A local nature reserve is looking for part-time volunteers to help them out during the summer holidays. You decide to apply. Write your letter of application.
>
> Your letter should include: • who you are
>   • why you would like to volunteer
>   • why you think you're right for the job

If the question has bullet points make sure you include all of them in your answer.

① Your <u>introduction</u> should be one paragraph saying what you're going to be writing about.

② Write down the points you want to make. Use <u>examples</u> to back them up.

③ <u>Sum up</u> your points then make a general statement to <u>finish</u> your answer.

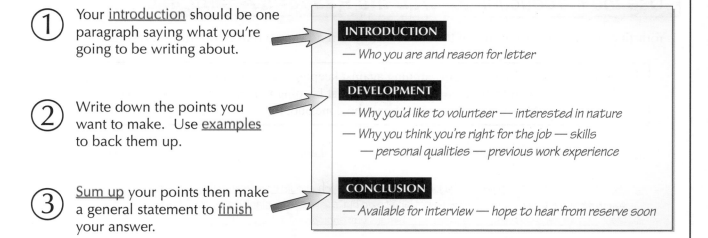

INTRODUCTION
— *Who you are and reason for letter*

DEVELOPMENT
— *Why you'd like to volunteer — interested in nature*
— *Why you think you're right for the job — skills*
    — *personal qualities — previous work experience*

CONCLUSION
— *Available for interview — hope to hear from reserve soon*

A good plan means you won't be tempted to ramble in your essay...

Writing that <u>rambles on</u> without getting anywhere <u>isn't</u> going to get you good marks.
All this needs to be <u>second nature</u> by the time you get to the exam, so get <u>learning</u>.

Starting Your Answer

You need to write a <u>clear</u> and <u>punchy introduction</u> to your answer — no waffle allowed.

Start with a *Good Introduction*

Introduce the <u>overall point</u> that your essay is making — and do it clearly.

> The introduction gives a <u>brief answer</u> to the question. The rest of the essay goes into more <u>depth</u>, and gives <u>evidence</u> to back up your points.

Your introduction should **Tell** *the reader* **What** *your essay is* **About**

> 1. Compare the texts 'Antipodean Adventures' and 'My Journey Across Australia' using the following headings: • the presentation of the text
>   • the layout of the text

Use <u>similar wording</u> to the question to link your answer to the question.

Explain the <u>effect</u> on the <u>reader</u>.

'Antipodean Adventures' and 'My Journey Across Australia' both use presentation and layout for effect. 'Antipodean Adventures' uses bright colours to appeal to younger readers. 'My Journey Across Australia' has a more formal layout to suit its adult audience.

<u>Clear</u> argument.

Use the introduction to **Grab the Reader's Attention**

Your first paragraph should make the reader want to read on, so make sure it's interesting.

> 2. Write an article for a magazine arguing against keeping wild animals in zoos. The article should include: • why you think that keeping wild animals in zoos is wrong
>   • what should be done about it

<u>Imaginative</u> beginning to interest the reader.

Language appeals to the reader's <u>emotions</u>.

Put yourself in his shoes: you're the king of the jungle — you should be running wild and free. Instead you're pacing a tiny concrete cell with nothing to do but stare at the blank walls. How would you feel? Yes we need to protect endangered animals, but shouldn't we find a better way?

Refers to the <u>opposite point of view</u>.

Asks <u>questions</u> to draw the reader in.

A good introduction will really impress the examiner...

The <u>introduction</u> is very important — it sets the <u>scene</u> for the rest of your answer. A really good, <u>attention-grabbing</u> one will make your reader want to read on — a dull one won't.

Paragraphs

Here's a little secret from me to you — <u>use paragraphs properly</u> if you want to get a decent grade.

Paragraphs make your writing Clearer

1) A <u>paragraph</u> is a group of sentences. These sentences are usually about the same thing.

2) Start a new paragraph every time there's a <u>change</u>.

> The street was quiet and very dark. Alex walked on tiptoes, trying to make as little noise as possible. Suddenly Alex heard a faint noise. Could it be the dreaded peanut-butter monster?

The <u>ideas</u> in this paragraph are all about Alex walking down the street. When something new happens, you start a <u>new paragraph</u>.

Start a New Paragraph every time Something Changes

When You Write About a New Place

This is happening <u>somewhere else</u>.

> The playing fields were quiet and peaceful. There was no one around. Further down the valley, a huge cloud of dust rose into the sky.

When You Talk About a New Person

A new paragraph for a <u>new person</u>.

> Liam sat on the edge of the stage, thinking about his guitar. Then he saw Keith. Keith was a skinny, ill-looking boy.

When You Start Writing About a Different Time

This has gone forward to a <u>different time</u>.

> By five o'clock, Edwin was angry. Shirley was late again. Six o'clock came, and still she didn't appear. Enough was enough.

Each Time a New Person Speaks

Someone new is <u>speaking</u>.

> "I'll find him," muttered Donald. "He won't get away." "What makes you so sure?" asked Mickey.

When You Start Writing About a New Topic

This is <u>another reason</u> why smoking is bad.

> It's widely known that smoking is bad for your health. It can lead to cancer and an early death. In addition, smoking is an expensive habit. Cigarette prices rise all the time but people will always pay.

It's important to make <u>one clear point</u> in each paragraph.

Changing paragraphs — any time, any place...

Remember, start a <u>new paragraph</u> whenever you change the person speaking, the people, the place or the time. Or whenever you make a <u>new point</u>. It's very important, that one.

Paragraphs

Once you've got your <u>paragraphs</u> sorted, you've got to make sure they <u>flow</u> properly.

Paragraphs need to be **Linked Together**

Use words and phrases like these to make the link clear:

- Therefore...
- However...
- For the same reason...
- On the other hand...
- Again...

These words clearly link the paragraphs together:

> ... free school meals for all pupils would mean that everyone got one healthy meal a day
>
> <u>However</u>, some people say that free school meals would be too expensive...

> ... people like the Scouts and yoga groups use the town hall every week.
>
> <u>Therefore</u>, I feel it would be a very bad idea to close the town hall...

Paragraphs should **Follow** a **Clear Order**

1) Make sure your paragraphs have a <u>clear order</u>.

2) It's up to you how you do it — just make sure it <u>makes sense</u>.

- Put your paragraphs in order of <u>importance</u>.
- Give paragraphs <u>for</u> an argument then paragraphs <u>against</u>.
- Put your paragraphs <u>in time order</u>.

Try to **Vary The Style** of your paragraphs

<u>Don't</u> make all of your paragraphs exactly the <u>same</u>. Here are a few tips for <u>spicing</u> things up a bit...

You could repeat sentence structures:

> Johnny was glad he was at the farm. <u>At school</u>, he felt like he didn't belong. <u>At home</u>, all he ever seemed to do was get in the way. But <u>at the farm</u>, Johnny came to life.

Or start with a rhetorical question (see p.37):

> <u>Is a world filled with violence and fear really the one we want our children to grow up in?</u>

Paragraphs — they do more than you think...

Paragraphs give <u>structure</u> to your answer and break it into <u>separate</u> points so it's easier to read. Excellent news. You can also use them <u>creatively</u> to make your work that bit more <u>interesting</u>.

Formal and Informal Language

As a general rule, use <u>formal language</u> unless you're writing to friends or young people.

Write in Formal Language

1)   Use <u>formal language</u> to speak or write to people you <u>don't know</u>. This includes your <u>examiner</u>.

2)   You should use <u>formal language</u> in most of your essays.

3)   When you use formal language, be accurate and <u>to the point</u>. Don't be chatty — that means <u>no slang</u>:

> I reckon Lady Macbeth wore the trousers in that household — she wasn't half bossy to her old man.   ✗

> Lady Macbeth was a forceful character, who had a strong influence over her husband.   ✓

4)   Use correct <u>punctuation</u>, <u>grammar</u> and <u>spelling</u> (see Section 9).

5)   <u>Don't</u> say "I" this and "I" that — just talk about the question, the text, the characters, the style, etc.

> I̶ ̶t̶h̶i̶n̶k̶ ̶t̶h̶a̶t̶ ͭʰᵉ language in the poem creates a sad mood. For example, I̶ ̶b̶e̶l̶i̶e̶v̶e̶ ̶t̶h̶a̶t̶ the image of the white blossom turning brown shows how their love has been ruined.

Only use Informal Language when it Suits The Task

1)   Use <u>informal language</u> if you're writing to <u>friends</u>, people you <u>know well</u> or <u>teenagers</u>. It's <u>chattier</u> and more <u>relaxed</u> than formal language, but it <u>doesn't</u> mean you can use <u>text speak</u>.

2)   Here's an example from a talk for teenagers about the internet:

Informal language is more suited to this audience than formal language.

> ... I'm not saying the internet isn't useful, but <u>how many hours have you lost watching X-factor hopefuls make fools of themselves on YouTube when you really should be researching your history project?</u>

You still need to use fancy writing tricks to get the marks though. This is a <u>rhetorical question</u> — see p.37.

You have to know how to use formal language...

So basically, you've almost always got to use <u>formal language</u> in your writing.
That means <u>proper</u> spelling, punctuation and grammar and absolutely <u>no slang</u>.

Giving Evidence and Quoting

You have to give <u>evidence</u> for everything you say or you'll <u>miss out</u> on loads of marks.

Give an **Example** every time you make a **Point**

You've got to show that you know what you're talking about — give <u>examples</u> for what you write.

> The woman was cruel to her dog.

This answer <u>doesn't</u> give any reasons...

...but this answer gives <u>examples</u> to back up the point it makes. That's loads better.

> The woman was cruel to her dog. She kept him chained up in the sun all day, with very little food and no water.

Use **Quotes** from other people

1) <u>Quoting</u> means using someone else's words to back up your arguments.

2) To quote someone <u>in their own words</u>, put <u>quotation marks</u> (" ") around what they're saying. This separates the other person's words from yours.

The quotation marks separate <u>your</u> words...

...from <u>Mr. Wright's</u> words.

> <u>Mr. Wright claimed that</u> "there was no other possible course of action."

Tips for using <u>quotation marks</u>:
- Use <u>exactly</u> the same words and punctuation as the person you're quoting.
- <u>Don't</u> make the quote <u>too long</u>.

3) If you put something <u>into your own words</u>, you don't need quotation marks:

> Mrs. Priya says, "Reading greatly improves vocabulary."

Direct quote

> Mrs. Priya claims that a good way to improve vocabulary is through reading.

In your own words

Writing must Flow around Quotes

Put your <u>quotes</u> in so the words around them still <u>make sense</u> and <u>flow</u> well:

> Mr Jones said, "Getting children interested in drama is important to us." The board has agreed to pay for drama workshops.

"Quotes are great," said CGP...

If you use loads of good <u>quotes</u>, you'll definitely improve your grade. Just <u>remember</u>, if you're quoting to <u>support</u> a point, explain <u>why</u> your quote backs it up. See p.14 for more about this.

Concluding

You've got to <u>conclude</u> your answer — but it shouldn't be a last-minute rushed job.

Bring together the **Key Points** in your **Conclusion**

You need to be able to <u>finish off</u> your essay <u>properly</u> — and that means writing a good conclusion.

> 1. Write an article for a student magazine explaining why backpacking is popular as a form of travel.

1) Start a new paragraph and conclude by going back to the <u>question</u>.

2) Go over the <u>main points</u> of your answer. Don't add any <u>new points</u>. They should be in the <u>main part</u> of your essay.

> For many people, backpacking is the best way to travel round different countries. It lets you travel wherever you want, and it's great for meeting interesting people. It is also the cheapest way of travelling, so people are more likely to be able to afford a visit to places that are far away. It's good to know that people don't need all their luxuries when they travel.

3) Once you've summed up, write one last sentence to <u>finish</u>.

There are lots of **Different Ways** to **Conclude**

1) You could give <u>advice</u> about what to do next:

> ... we must do something. We need to create more protected areas of woodland before it's too late.

2) You could ask the reader a <u>rhetorical question</u> (see p.37):

> ... so, do we take action or just sit back and do nothing? Is this the end of the world as we know it?

This gives the reader a chance to make up their own mind.

3) You could <u>go back</u> to the points you made in your introduction.

4) If you're using <u>formal</u> language, you could start your last paragraph with 'In conclusion...'.

Is this page important? Draw your own conclusions...

Always leave <u>time</u> in an exam to write your <u>conclusion</u>, even if it means writing less in another section. It's your chance to bring all your points <u>together</u> and show that you've answered the <u>question</u>.

Checking

You've got five minutes left in the exam... time to read through your work.

Check Over your Essay when you've Finished

1) Check the grammar, spelling and punctuation. If you find a mistake, put brackets round it, cross it out neatly with two lines through it and write the correction above.

Macbeth
(McBath)

2) If you've written something which isn't clear, put a star * at the end of the sentence. Put another star at the end of your answer, and write what you mean beside it.

* something I forgot

3) If you realise you should have started a new paragraph, put "//" to show where it starts.

4) If you find you've missed out a word or two, put one of these: "∧" where the words should go, then write them in above the line.

Don't Panic if you realise you've Gone Wrong in an Exam

If you realise you've forgotten something obvious, then add it in — even if it's at the bottom of the final page. You might get marks for noticing your mistake.

Never cross out your whole answer if you realise it's wrong. If you've got time left, explain what the real answer is.

Always chck yoor worke...

Mistakes are easy to make, especially in exam conditions, so you must give yourself time to check things over. Don't panic if you've gone wrong — there are plenty of ways to fix it.

Revision Summary

Every now and then throughout this book, you'll find pages like this one.
They may look dull, but they're really important, so <u>don't skip them.</u>

You've read the section, but can you remember it? Here's where you find out — right here, right now.

Do <u>all</u> these questions without cheating, then turn back and look up the bits you didn't know.
Check them, and do the <u>whole lot again</u> until you get 100% correct.

1) How long (roughly) should you spend planning each essay in the exam?

2) Your plan should cover the main three sections of your answer. The first of these sections is the introduction. What are the other two?

3) Why would you use similar wording to the question in your introduction?

4) How might your introduction grab the reader's attention?

5) Why should you write your answers using paragraphs?

6) Which of these would be a reason to start a new paragraph —
      a) when a new person speaks,
      b) when you write about a new place or a new time,
      c) when you're hungry?

7) Which of these words and phrases are generally good for linking paragraphs —
      a) However,
      b) I don't know,
      c) On the other hand,
      d) Horses?

8) Which would be better — to order your paragraphs from longest to shortest or in order of importance?

9) Give an example of how you could vary the style of your paragraphs.

10) What does 'formal writing' mean?

11) Which of the following would you write in informal language —
      a) a letter to your MP,
      b) a postcard to your friend,
      c) an article on clothes for a teenage magazine?

12) Why do you need to give examples for the points you make?

13) Do you need quotation marks when you put what someone else has said into your own words?

14) Which of these would make a good conclusion —
      a) advice about what to do next,
      b) a brand new point,
      c) a summary of the points you made in your introduction,
      d) your reader's horoscope?

15) Explain why you need to leave yourself time at the end of the exam to check through your answer.

16) What's the best thing to do if you realise that you've forgotten to include something important in your exam answer?

Reading the Question

A <u>non-fiction</u> text is anything that's about <u>real life</u>, like a newspaper article or a leaflet.

Three Things to get you Marks in Non-Fiction Text exams

These are all things that the examiner wants to give you marks for:

1) Showing that you've <u>understood</u> and thought about the texts, and that you can <u>compare</u> them.
2) Showing that you can pick out <u>facts</u> from the text and <u>explain</u> them.
3) Explaining how <u>language</u> and <u>how the text looks</u> can influence the reader.

<u>Don't panic</u> — this section will show you how to do all these things.

If you're doing Edexcel, non-fiction texts could be part of a controlled assessment or an exam.

Read the Question Before the Text

Look at the question <u>before</u> you start — it'll tell you what to look out for.

Pick out the <u>key words</u> in each question and <u>underline</u> them.

> 1. <u>Compare</u> how the writers use <u>language</u> to <u>influence the reader</u> in 'The Future of Our Planet: Should We Be Building an Ark?' and 'End of the World? I don't think so.'

> 2. <u>What reasons</u> can you find in the newspaper article for saying that Jimmy Jones is both a <u>successful singer</u> and <u>a helpful person</u>?

Think about How Much the question is Worth

1) The questions are worth <u>different amounts</u> of marks.
   The number of marks for each question will be written on the exam paper.
2) Make sure you know what the <u>total number of marks</u> is.
   Then you can decide how much of the <u>total time</u> to spend on each question.
3) Don't spend <u>half</u> the exam answering a question worth <u>4 marks</u> if the next question's worth <u>8 marks</u>.

What's the question worth? — I'll give you £5 and a lemon bonbon...

Spend <u>less time</u> on questions that are worth <u>fewer marks</u> — simple really. And remember, what the examiner really wants is for you to show you've <u>understood the text</u>. Do that and you're laughing.

Reading the Text and Making Notes

No one likes making notes, but they stop you rambling on in your essays.

You might need to **Pick Out Facts** from the text

Questions which ask you to pick out facts only need short answers.

1) A question may ask you to find and write down some bits of information from the text.
2) Read the question really carefully and only write down things the question asks for.
3) Look at the number of marks the question is worth. This tells you how many facts to pick out.

For some questions, your answer booklet might have a blank numbered list for you to fill in — if it does, don't leave any spaces.

Find the bits that **Answer** the **Question**

After you've read the question, go through each text at least twice, slowly and carefully.
Pick out the important bits that will help you answer the question.

What are the writer's thoughts and feelings towards Ben Kilham's approach?
Your answer should include:
- whether or not he agrees with it
- what other people think
- his overall impression.

Some questions won't give you bullet points like this.

GENTLE BEN

Most people try not to get too close to wild bears. Not Ben Kilham. When two injured bears were brought to his animal park, he brought them home and looked after them in his guest room. "It didn't take long for them to trust me," he says, "They used to follow me round the house." Some experts worry that treating bears this way will make them too tame. However, Kilham cared for three cubs last year and they now live happily in the animal park with the other bears.

Underline key points as you read and jot down some notes on the exam paper.

Key point — Includes Ben's own words — shows the writer thinks what Ben says is important and suggests he agrees with him.

Key point — Shows what other people think about Ben's approach — makes the article seem more balanced.

Key point — The writer provides another argument which supports Ben's approach.

Write notes as you read and focus on the question...

The examiners want to know you've understood the text. When you're picking points out, make sure you're only writing down things that the question asks for. Anything else is just a waste of time.

Longer Answers

The next two pages will give you the skills you'll need to write <u>longer</u>, more <u>detailed</u> answers.

Try to sound **Confident**

Use your own words to explain the question and then say what your argument's going to be.

Key words.

How does the writer of 'Careless Talk' use language to make the article <u>informative</u> and <u>interesting</u>?

'Careless Talk' is informative and interesting because of the language used.

This is <u>dull</u> — it repeats exactly what's in the question and won't get you any extra marks.

This is much <u>better</u>. It still links to the question but explains how the writer uses language.

'Careless Talk' uses quotes and stories from real people to inform the reader and keep them interested.

Back up your points with **Examples**

1) For questions that need longer answers, back up your points with <u>evidence</u>.
2) This will usually be a <u>quote</u> (see p.8), but it could be a description of the pictures or layout.
3) <u>Explain</u> what your example shows about the text.

These examples are about the <u>presentation</u> of the text.

The leaflet is designed to appeal to young children. <u>For example, it uses bright colours and simple fonts</u>. <u>This makes the leaflet look friendly and fun</u>.

This explains <u>why</u> the writer chose a certain <u>style</u>.

So, here's what a good essay answer should do:

1) Make <u>points</u> to answer the question you've been given.
2) Give <u>examples</u> from the text (either a quote or a description).
3) <u>Explain</u> how your examples back up your point.

This is really important — keep <u>developing</u> your answer.

Don't bury examiners with lots of detail...

OK, so you get the message — be <u>confident</u>, use your <u>own words</u>, <u>back up</u> your arguments and add an explanation. Examiners can always spot waffle, so stick to the <u>point</u> and you'll get lots of marks.

Longer Answers

There are <u>plenty</u> of ways you can <u>develop</u> your answer — there's <u>more</u> to it than adding quotes.

Some questions ask about **Thoughts** and **Feelings**

You may understand the facts a writer gives you, but some questions will ask for <u>more</u>.

1) Try to work out how the writer <u>feels</u> about what they're describing. For example:

> There is a strong sense that the writer <u>feels angry</u> about the changes.

2) You could show you understand <u>what</u> the writer wants readers to <u>think about</u>. For example:

> The article <u>makes the reader question</u> whether schools are a good thing.

3) You could comment on how the <u>writer</u> tries to make <u>readers</u> feel. For example:

> The writer seems <u>to want to make readers feel guilty</u>.

Some questions will ask about the writer's language — there's more about this in <u>Section 3</u>.

Compare and **Contrast** the texts

1) You might get a question asking you to <u>compare</u> texts.
This means picking out the <u>differences</u> and <u>similarities</u> between them. E.g.:

Some questions might not give you bullet points to help you.

> Now look again at all three items.
> They have each been written in an interesting way.
>
> **1.** Choose **two** of these items. Compare them using these headings:
> *   the writers' intended audiences
> *   the ways in which the writers use language.

2) If you're given <u>headings</u> or <u>bullet points</u>, write about all of them and write about the <u>same amount</u> for each.

3) <u>Plan</u> your answer before you start. If you're given <u>headings</u>, include points about each one in your <u>plan</u>.

4) Try to write an <u>equal amount</u> about both texts. Keep <u>making links</u> between them in your answer.

Writers write that way for a reason...

Some questions will ask you to consider less obvious things like the <u>writer's thoughts</u> and <u>ideas</u>.
Be <u>confident</u> — if you think the writer feels a certain way, say so and then find some <u>evidence</u>.

Writing about the Format of a Non-Fiction Text

There's <u>lots</u> to think about when it comes to non-fiction texts, including the way the text <u>looks</u>.

It's **Not Just Words** you need to think about

1) The <u>texts</u> in the exam could be magazine or newspaper articles, or printed adverts.

2) You need to comment on the <u>format</u> of what you're given — think about things like the overall <u>presentation</u>, the <u>layout</u> of the text and the way <u>graphics</u> are used.

'Format' means the way the writing and pictures are organised to make a text look a certain way.

Think about what the **Graphics** are trying to **Do**

1) Texts often have graphics, e.g. photos, pictures, diagrams.
2) They might have <u>captions</u> with them — a short bit of text to explain what the graphic shows.
3) All graphics have a <u>purpose</u>, e.g. photos can show <u>real-life</u> examples of what's in the text. It's no good just saying that there are three photos. Instead <u>describe</u> them and <u>explain</u> their effect.

Mention the **Layout**

Different layouts are used for different <u>audiences</u>.

This layout is <u>serious</u>. There's hardly any colour, most of the text is the same size and the picture is formal. It's probably aimed at <u>adults</u>.

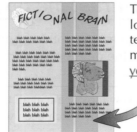

This layout is more <u>fun</u>. There's lots of colour, more space, the text size is varied, the picture is more entertaining. It's aimed at <u>young people</u>.

Talk about **Headlines** too

1) Headlines tell you <u>what</u> the article is <u>about</u> in a few words. They're there to grab your <u>attention</u>, so you'll read the article.
2) Headlines are usually <u>bigger</u> and at the <u>top</u> of the page.
3) They can use <u>humour</u> or <u>shocking facts</u> to get your attention.

This is the headline.

Look at every part of a non-fiction text — not just the writing...

<u>Graphics</u> will pop up all the time, so just use your common sense to <u>explain</u> what you can see. Think about what <u>kind</u> of graphic it is, <u>why</u> you think it's there and the <u>effect</u> it has.

Warm-Up and Exam Questions

People often find non-fiction texts a bit tricky, but if you've paid attention to this section, these warm-up questions should be OK. When you've warmed up, there are some bigger beasts for you to try — practice exam questions. Don't worry — they won't bite. The non-fiction texts are on pages 18-20, and on page 21 we've thrown in a worked exam answer to Question 4, too.

Warm-Up Questions

1. Questions about non-fiction texts are great because you don't need to quote from the text to back up your answers *True or False*?

2. Is it best to read the question before or after you read the text? Why?

3. Why is it a good idea to underline key words in the question?

4. How can you make it really obvious that you're answering the question in your first sentence?

Exam Questions

Read **Item 1**, the website article called 'Fireworks and animals' and answer the questions below.

1. List four things the leaflet tells you about how to prepare for bonfire night if you have animals.

    (4 marks)

2. According to the article, why is it important to look after animals on bonfire night?

    (4 marks)

Read **Item 2**, the newspaper article called 'British teenager becomes youngest person to sail round the world solo' and answer the question below.

3. What reasons can you find in the article for saying that Mike Perham had both "amazing" experiences and difficult times during his expedition?

    (8 marks)

Read **Item 3**, the Habitat for Humanity article called 'When Danger Starts at Home' and answer the question below.

4. How does the writer use language to inform the reader and persuade them to donate money?

    (12 marks)

Now look again at all three items. They have each been presented in an interesting way.

5. Choose **two** of these items. Compare them using these headings:
    - the use of titles and subtitles
    - the use of pictures.

    (12 marks)

Item 1

Fireworks and animals

How to keep your pets safe

Fireworks and animals

Every year thousands of animals will suffer as a result of fireworks being let off. Blue Cross animal hospitals across the country see a marked rise in pets requiring medication during such stressful times, and many animals are brought into Blue Cross adoption centres having run away from home.

Animals have very acute hearing. Loud bangs and whistles may cause them actual pain in their ears. But by following these simple guidelines your pet need not suffer.

Small pets

Rabbits, guinea pigs, hamsters, gerbils, mice, ferrets and birds all need to be treated with special care when fireworks are being let off. These animals are easily frightened. The Blue Cross advises that owners of such types of small animal should follow these precautions.

- Give your pet extra bedding to burrow into so it feels safe.

- Hutches/cages and enclosures should, if possible, be brought into a quiet room indoors, or into a garage or shed.

- If you cannot bring your pet's hutch inside, you should turn its enclosure around so that it faces a wall or fence instead of the open garden.

- Cover any aviaries or hutches with thick blankets or a duvet to block out the sight of the fireworks and deaden the sound of the bangs, but make sure there is enough ventilation.

Dogs & cats

- Always keep dogs and cats inside when fireworks are being let off. Make sure your dog is walked earlier in the day before the fireworks start.

- Close all windows and doors, and block off catflaps to stop pets escaping and to keep noise to a minimum. Draw the curtains, and if the animals are used to the sounds of TV or radio, switch them on (but not too loudly) in order to block out some of the noise of the fireworks.

- Ensure dogs are wearing some form of easily readable identification (ID) – even in the house. They should have at least a collar and tag. Think about fitting pets with a microchip, so that if they do run away they have a better chance of being quickly reunited with you.

- Prepare a 'den' for your pet where it can feel safe and comfortable – perhaps under a bed with some of your old clothes. It may like to hide there when the fireworks start.

Item 2

British teenager becomes youngest person to sail round the world solo

Nine months after setting sail from Portsmouth in his Open 50 racing yacht, 17-year-old Mike Perham returns home

Caroline Davies

The Guardian, 27 August 2009

Mike Perham on his return to Portsmouth

Nine months, some 30,000 miles, and several euphemistic* "Oh crikey!" moments after leaving Portsmouth, British teenager Mike Perham, 17, today became the youngest person to sail solo around the globe.

The college student from land-locked Hertfordshire crossed the finishing line between Lizard Point and Ushant in France at 9.47am after braving 50ft waves, gale-force winds and a couple of hair-raising "knockdowns" during his voyage into the record books. "I am absolutely ecstatic*. It feels amazing," he said from his Open 50 racing yacht, TotallyMoney.com. "I am really looking forward to seeing my family and friends, getting back to my own house, and especially getting into my own bed at last."

Setting off as a 16-year-old, equipped with an iPod, "icky" freeze-dried food supplies and a couple of robust laptops from which to blog, Mike's intention was to complete his circumnavigation* non-stop in under five months. But those hairy moments, which saw his auto-pilot then his rudder fail, winds that shredded his sail and towering waves, forced him to pull in for repairs. Stops in Portugal, Gran Canaria, Cape Town, Tasmania and New Zealand threw him behind schedule and forced him through the Panama Canal rather than round Cape

Horn. It also meant he had to abandon his attempt at a non-stop, non-assisted circumnavigation. "It was a bit of a disappointment. But I always knew there was a chance of stopping," he said.

Horrendous weather in the Southern Ocean saw 50ft waves in 50-knot winds, and necessitated mast repairs after two knockdowns*. Another drama found him cutting ropes tangled on the rudder by diving under the boat in 30-second dives for 40 minutes in the Pacific.

"There are lows, but the ongoing low is that you are on your own, totally," he said yesterday via satellite phone. "That's not nice, but it is part of the challenge. I never thought about giving up. Though sometimes you do ask yourself, Why on earth am I doing it?

"There were so many experiences I will never forget. Seeing hundreds of dolphins at once, or seeing whales next to you. There were some incredible sunsets and some beautifully clear days."

Sleeping in half-hour snatches, he avoided pirates in the Caribbean by turning off his tracking system, and dodged tankers around Panama, while continuing his studies for a sports diploma. Twice daily satellite calls to his father, Peter, 49, his mother, Heather, 51, and his sister, Fiona, 18, at home in Potters Bar helped ease his solitude*. With his iPod on shuffle, and featuring favourite bands U2 and the Black Eyed Peas, his days were spent repairing, and stuffing himself with rice and pasta.

He cracked open champagne twice – on his 17th birthday on 16 March, and on crossing the equator. It is not his first record. At 14 he became the youngest to cross the Atlantic single-handed.

His father, who joined him today, said: "Mike is a very special son. He has done incredibly well and shown that with determination you can succeed in the most adverse* circumstances."

*euphemistic — describing upsetting words in a more polite way

*circumnavigation — a sailing voyage around the world

*knockdowns — when a boat is knocked over so that it lies flat in the water

* solitude — loneliness

* adverse — difficult

* ecstatic — very happy

When Danger Starts at Home

Please help me get families like Hector's out of the derelict apartments and into decent homes – for good.

Hector lives in "La Boca", a dangerous neighbourhood in the City of Buenos Aires. Home for Hector's family is a crumbling, rusting apartment block with his dad Jorge, his mum Estela (who is deaf and mute), his sisters Claudia and Viviana (eleven year old twins) and brother Victor.

The very structure of the apartment block is dangerous and a tragedy waiting to happen. Every step you take is followed by a cracking sound and Jorge has to warn his youngest son not to jump inside the house. Why? Because he might go through the floor.

© Oliver Kornblihtt

The family faces many dangers each day, just from living in the apartment block. The neighbourhood is full of such tenement* buildings, all of which are prone to fires.

© Oliver Kornblihtt

Hector's family has to be very careful with the lights and gas supply because the building is so dilapidated*. One mistake could mean the destruction of the whole structure, or worse.

Why do so many families like Hector's live amid such daily dangers? Because they have no choice.

There is a massive housing deficit* in Argentina, and thousands upon thousands of families have no choices except living on the street, in abandoned factories, or in derelict apartments.

These derelict apartments come with a price beyond the danger. Because they are in such poor condition, it is illegal to let them out, so their unscrupulous* owners take advantage of desperate families. There are no terms; there is no legal recourse*; and the families have no leg to stand on. But they are desperate so they pay the money, knowing full well that they might be evicted at any moment.

So the choice really is: do you want your family to live on the streets, or not? Is it better to risk life in this apartment than life on the streets?

Thankfully, this terrible choice can come to an end. There is another way for these families. Together we can offer more and more families in these illegal and rundown apartments a way out. We need your help to renovate the future for hundreds of families like Hector's.

You can be a part of this solution for Hector and hundreds of others like him. Your gift will help us transform the lives of families like Hector's. Hector's family should not have to suffer the dangers of a crumbling, rotting apartment; what they need is a safe, decent home.

---

*tenement — a run-down apartment block

*dilapidated — run down

*deficit — shortage

*unscrupulous — unfair

*legal recourse — getting the law to help

Worked Exam Answer

To help you get to grips with these non-fiction reading texts exam questions, I've cooked up a little exam answer to give you some pointers. Enjoy.

Worked Exam Answer

Read **Item 3**, the Habitat for Humanity article called 'When Danger Starts at Home' and answer the question below.

4) How does the writer use language to inform the reader and persuade them to donate money?

(12 marks)

Inform

This article uses informative language to show how bad things are for Hector and his family, and for thousands of people like him, and how we can act to help them. By focusing on one family the writer can show the problems that they face, while talking about a problem that affects "thousands" of people. This makes it <u>easier for the reader to understand how the problem affects people</u>.

Try to show how the language used helps to inform the reader.

The writer uses technical language to describe the situation, for example "housing deficit" and "legal recourse". This tells the reader facts about the situation and how serious it is. It also makes the writer seem well informed.

The writer makes it clear to the reader that their help is needed, by using words like "<u>you</u>" and "<u>we</u>". This makes it clear that the main purpose of the article is to show how the reader can help people like Hector, for example by referring to "your help" and "your gift".

When you're writing about the language, mention the particular words used.

Persuade

The writer uses <u>emotive</u> language to show that the housing problem in Buenos Aires affects individuals. He does this by telling the story of one family. By giving details of the family members such as names and ages, we are made to sympathise with them directly and want to donate money to help improve their living conditions.

'Emotive' is a good word — it means it's trying to get the reader to feel strongly.

The writer uses vivid descriptive language to describe the family living in "<u>a crumbling, rusting apartment block</u>". This helps the reader to picture how bad it is, which makes us feel sorry for them and want to help.

Try to put in a short quote for nearly every point.

The writer describes their home as "a tragedy waiting to happen." This dramatic language makes it seem like helping them is really urgent, as if something terrible might happen if they don't move into better housing. <u>This means the reader is more likely to donate money straight away</u>.

Think about what effect the language will have on the reader.

Revision Summary

Non-fiction texts don't have to be tricky. Just remember to read them with the question in mind so you know what to look out for. That way you can underline the key points and it'll be a breeze when you come to writing the answer.

Have a go at these questions on Section Two. If you get stuck, don't worry, just go back and read that page again, then have another go at the question.

1) If a question asks you to pick out some facts from the text, why is it important to look at the number of marks the question is worth?

2) Is there any other reason why it might be useful to note how many marks a question is worth?

3) What kind of first impression do you want your answer to make on the examiner?

4) When you make a point in an essay, what should you back it up with:
   a) nothing — you don't have the time
   b) examples from the text
   c) a comfortable cushion?

5) Other than facts, what else could you think about when writing about a text:
   a) how the writer feels about the subject
   b) what you think they had for breakfast
   c) what the writer wants the reader to think about?

6) If you're asked to compare and contrast, what should you do:
   a) write about the similarities and differences between the texts
   b) just write about one text in detail and ignore the other one
   c) rock backwards and forwards on your chair in a mad panic?

7) What is meant by the 'format' of a text?

8) List three different kinds of graphics that you might find in a non-fiction text.

9) What is the purpose of a caption?

10) Is it important to think about the layout of a non-fiction text? Why?

11) What is the main purpose of a headline?

Different Forms

Non-fiction texts come in many <u>different forms</u>. The next two pages cover the main ones.

Letters *can be* **Formal** *or* **Informal**

1) <u>Informal letters</u> are the kind of letters that you'd send to a friend.
   Use a <u>chatty style</u> if it suits the reader, but stick to <u>Standard English</u> (see p.92).

2) <u>Formal letters</u>, e.g. job applications, need a more <u>serious</u> tone and language.

3) Give letters a clear <u>structure</u>, e.g. a greeting at the beginning and a suitable ending.

4) Letters can have many different <u>purposes</u> (see p.26). E.g.:

> • <u>informing</u> — gives readers information e.g. a letter to a newspaper about a fund-raising event.
>
> • <u>persuading</u> — gets someone to do something e.g. a letter to a friend persuading them to visit you.

Newspaper *and* **Magazine** *articles should be* **Factual**

For <u>newspaper</u> or <u>magazine articles</u>, you only need to write the <u>text</u>, so don't worry about <u>layout</u>.

1) You need to give <u>facts</u> and <u>evidence</u> — e.g. quotes (see p.8) and statistics.

2) Use <u>headlines</u> and <u>subheadings</u> to break up the writing.

3) Articles can have different <u>purposes</u>, e.g.:

Articles can have more than one purpose.

> • <u>informing</u> — e.g. a newspaper article telling people about an upcoming event.
>
> • <u>explaining</u> — e.g. a car magazine might explain the features of a new family car.

The <u>language</u> and <u>tone</u> of an article depends on its <u>purpose</u> and <u>audience</u>.

Leaflets *are usually short*

Leaflets can <u>inform</u>, <u>advise</u> or put across an <u>argument</u>.

1) If you're writing a leaflet, don't spend <u>time</u> making it look <u>pretty</u> or drawing <u>pictures</u>.

2) Leaflets should <u>catch people's attention</u> and <u>give information</u> clearly.

3) Use <u>headings</u> and <u>bullet points</u> to break up the text.

4) This is the <u>kind</u> of question you could get:

> Write the text of a leaflet which informs tourists of what your area has to offer them.

I'll keep this short and sweet — revise...

Letters, newspaper articles and leaflets can be about <u>almost anything</u>. If you have to write one
of these texts in the exam, <u>read the question</u> carefully to find out <u>who</u> you're writing for, and <u>why</u>.

Different Forms

You want <u>more types</u> of non-fiction text — you've come to the right place.

Reviews are Round-Ups of information

<u>Reviews</u> describe something, e.g. a film, and say what is (or isn't) great about it.

1) Reviews can be <u>formal</u> or <u>informal</u>. Their purpose is to <u>inform</u> (see p.26) and give an <u>opinion</u>.
2) <u>Include some facts</u> — your audience needs to know <u>exactly</u> what it is you're writing about.
3) Write <u>confidently</u>. Show your audience that you know what you're talking about.

> For example, you might write a <u>review</u> of:
> * a hotel   * a restaurant   * a book   * a play or film

See p.44 for more on reviews

Talks and Speeches are designed to be Spoken

For talks or speeches you need to make the words <u>easy to remember</u>.

1) Write in a style that would <u>sound good</u> to a room full of listeners.
2) The tone might be <u>formal</u> or <u>informal</u> (see p.7), depending on your audience.
3) Include some <u>interesting language</u> and <u>techniques</u> (see p.37).
4) Give your speech a <u>clear structure</u>, e.g. <u>start with a short introduction</u> to the topic and <u>finish by reminding</u> the audience what they've just been told.

Make your writing Organised and Interesting

Whatever form of text you're writing, you'll be marked on:

* how well you <u>organise</u> and <u>communicate</u> the information.
* the <u>quality</u> of your <u>writing</u>.

1) <u>Structure</u> your writing using <u>paragraphs</u> and link your <u>sentences</u> together.
2) <u>Sometimes</u> you can you use headings and bullet points, but make sure you write mostly in paragraphs.
3) Write in a way that'll <u>interest</u> your readers.

Speeches are designed to be spoken — not sung...

For any non-fiction text, the most <u>important</u> things to keep in mind are <u>why</u> you're writing the text and <u>who</u> you're writing it for. There's more advice on the next few pages.

Audience

Whatever <u>type</u> of text you're writing, keep in mind <u>who</u> you're writing for.

Think about who your Audience is

In exam questions, you may only be given vague information — you'll have to decide on the details.

1) <u>Who are you writing for?</u> You'll usually be given some idea of who your audience is:

> • <u>A manager of a business</u>. You might be trying to persuade them to employ you, so use formal language to make yourself sound professional.

> • <u>A friend</u>. You can be a bit more laid-back with your friends, but don't overdo it.

> • <u>Teenagers</u>. Your readers will be your age, but don't be too informal.

> • <u>Adults</u>. Be more formal with adults than you would with younger people.

2) Sometimes you won't get much detail about your audience. In this case, write for a <u>general audience</u> — not too technical or too informal.

3) Match the <u>content</u> of your writing to your audience. Choose details that will <u>interest</u> them.

Don't make Informal writing Too Simple

1) If the question asks you to write to a <u>friend</u>, don't write too casually and <u>never</u> use <u>text speak</u>.
2) You can sound <u>chatty</u> but make sure you still include a <u>range</u> of sentences and vocabulary.
3) You can be <u>sarcastic</u> or <u>humorous</u> to make your writing more interesting.

E.g. if you have to write a letter to a friend, this is the sort of thing you <u>should</u> write:

✔ 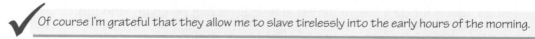 *Of course I'm grateful that they allow me to slave tirelessly into the early hours of the morning.*

But make sure you don't use <u>slang</u> or <u>text speak</u> like this:

✘  *Mate, here's some goss 4 ya. That guy from skool u like stank like 2 much BO 2day.*

You've been a wonderful audience...

When you email your real friends, your writing is probably really <u>informal</u>, simple and to the point. But when you write to a 'friend' in the exam you've got to remember to <u>show off</u> your writing at its <u>best</u>.

Purpose

Every piece of writing should have a purpose — that means why you're writing it.

Make sure your writing Achieves its Purpose

1) The purpose is your reason for writing. It tells you how your writing should affect your reader.

Some questions have more than one purpose.

2) Purposes (or reasons for writing) are:

Arguing, persuading...	... informing, explaining, advising...	and	describing.
see p.27-32	see p.33-36		see p.47

Exam questions often give you a big hint about the purpose of the piece. E.g.:

> Write a letter to a local business arguing that schools need more support and persuading them to help.

> Write a letter explaining what you do to represent your school at local youth group meetings.

3) Think about the purpose when you're planning. If you're given bullet points, cover all of them.

4) When you've finished writing, read through it and make sure the purpose is clear all the way through.

> E.g. If you're applying for a job, have you informed the reader of your talents, and persuaded them that you're the right person to employ?

Choose the right Language for the purpose

The language you use has to suit your purpose.

1) For example, a letter to the council should be formal and serious...

2) ... but an advert for spot cream aimed at teenagers can be chatty and fun.

3) No matter what you're writing, use a range of vocabulary.

4) Use lots of detail to suit your purpose. E.g. if you're writing to persuade, you could include some shocking statistics. If you're writing to describe, put in details from all five senses (see p.47).

I'd argue that it's time for an informative explanation...

Before you start writing, make sure you know the purpose of the piece. If you get it wrong and start persuading when you're supposed to be informing, you won't get the best marks.

Persuasive Writing — Structuring Your Answer

You need a good <u>argument</u> and truckloads of <u>evidence</u> to persuade your readers to agree with you.

Make sure your writing is **Structured**

1) <u>Work out a plan</u> — spend about five minutes making a plan like the one below.
2) <u>Don't repeat the same idea</u> — use the bullet points (if you're given some) to organise your ideas.
3) <u>Fill in the gaps</u> — once you've planned, try to fit in bits of evidence, facts, examples etc.

Plan *your persuasive answers around this* **Basic Structure**

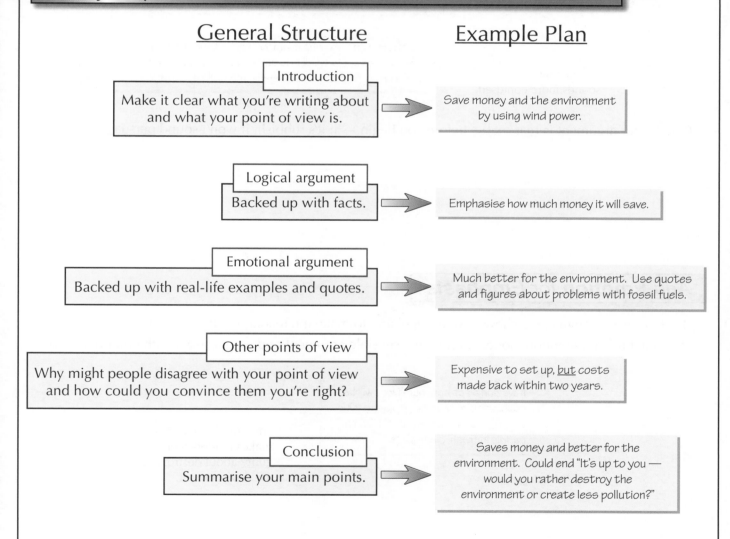

General Structure

Introduction
Make it clear what you're writing about and what your point of view is.

Logical argument
Backed up with facts.

Emotional argument
Backed up with real-life examples and quotes.

Other points of view
Why might people disagree with your point of view and how could you convince them you're right?

Conclusion
Summarise your main points.

Example Plan

Save money and the environment by using wind power.

Emphasise how much money it will save.

Much better for the environment. Use quotes and figures about problems with fossil fuels.

Expensive to set up, <u>but</u> costs made back within two years.

Saves money and better for the environment. Could end "It's up to you — would you rather destroy the environment or create less pollution?"

I love it when a plan comes together...

<u>Plan</u> what to write, and write what you <u>planned</u>. And remember, if you don't know any facts about the subject you're writing about, you can make them up. Try to make them sound <u>realistic</u> though.

Arguing or Persuading

This page contains a few cunning tricks that you can use to make your writing persuasive.

Use **Reason** to make your argument **Logical**

Your argument must make sense.

1) Show the reader that what you're arguing is the only reasonable point of view.
2) You don't have to agree with what you write. Just make sure you have a strong argument.
3) Use definite language (e.g. 'will', 'all') and sound confident.

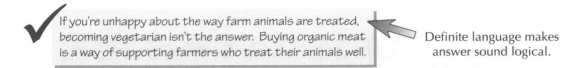

✓ If you're unhappy about the way farm animals are treated, becoming vegetarian isn't the answer. Buying organic meat is a way of supporting farmers who treat their animals well.

Definite language makes answer sound logical.

There's no strong argument here so it sounds more confused.

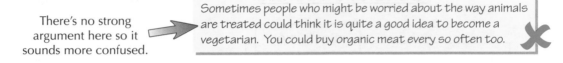

Sometimes people who might be worried about the way animals are treated could think it is quite a good idea to become a vegetarian. You could buy organic meat every so often too. ✗

Check your argument is reasonable before you begin — if it's rubbish, it won't sound persuasive.

Add **Emotion** for **Emphasis**

1) Use strong language to show how you feel and to make the reader feel the same way.
2) Don't rely on emotion alone. Start with a sensible argument and emphasise it with emotion.

If we don't act now, our rivers will be nothing more than dirty sludge. Our children won't know what it's like to paddle in fresh, clear water.

Emotional language makes readers feel guilty about destroying the environment.

Logic and emotion make a fantastic team...

Tug at people's heartstrings and they'll be putty in your hands. It's the oldest trick in the book. But don't get carried away — the moment you stop being realistic, you've lost them.

Arguing or Persuading

In <u>persuasive</u> writing, make sure you <u>back up</u> your arguments with facts, opinions and examples.

Say if you **Believe** something is **Right or Wrong**

1) Most people share certain beliefs about things that are <u>right and wrong</u>, e.g. 'poverty is bad'.

2) They <u>feel strongly</u> about these things, so it's a <u>good idea</u> to use them in your argument.

> Giving aid to poor nations is not enough, it is by cancelling their debts that we can really make a difference. In many cases debt is crippling their economies, keeping 80% of the population below the poverty line.

You don't actually need to say 'poverty is wrong' — you can assume that your readers will agree with that.

<u>Don't</u> get angry and start <u>ranting</u> in your exam answer and don't write anything that's too <u>over the top</u>.

> Only giving aid to poor nations isn't enough and you'd have to be stupid to disagree. We have to cancel their debt, otherwise we're keeping people poor which is just wrong.

Calm and logical arguments are more likely to <u>convince</u> someone that you're right, rather than just ranting.

Use facts **Carefully**

1) Don't get bogged down in <u>statistics</u>, especially in speeches.

2) Use <u>simple</u>, easy-to-understand facts.

3) This is especially important if you're writing the text for a <u>speech</u> — the people listening will doze off if you go into too much detail.

Confusing — too much detail.

> Using the Kid800 Wonderpen, 83% of children aged 7 years old wrote an average of 95 words at a speed of 1.58 words per minute.

This is a good statistic, because it's easy to understand.

> 83% of children could write more quickly when using the Kid800 Wonderpen.

75% of all facts are brilliant...

Facts are very useful for <u>backing up</u> your arguments and <u>convincing</u> the reader that you're right. Be careful though, they have to be <u>relevant</u> and used <u>properly</u> or they're just really confusing.

Arguing or Persuading

This page tells you about some great ways of backing up your argument.

Use *Opinions* from *Experts*

1) Use expert opinion to back up your arguments.
2) Say who the experts are and how they're related to your argument.
3) You can include expert opinions as quotes (see example below)
   or explain them in your own words (see p.8).

Don't forget that anything you make up must be realistic — don't claim that 100% of people prefer blue to green or quote an expert saying the world is made of soap.

Use *Relevant Quotations*

1) Make sure the quote is relevant.
2) Keep it short. Don't include long extracts.
3) Use quotation marks for direct (exact word) quotations and also say who you're quoting.

> Officer Robert Jones agrees, saying, "I've looked into these recent accidents and I can confirm they were all caused by bad weather."

Use *'Real-life' Examples*

1) Your argument should sound as though it's true in real-life.
2) Give examples that sound realistic to make your argument more convincing.
3) Choose examples that fit your argument as closely as possible.

> After initial concerns, a skate park was built within the main park. Youth crime has since dropped. This was a direct result of the park, according to local police officer Rose Leven. ✔

> The creation of a rose garden in the park has increased visitor numbers. This may have contributed to a reduction in youth crime in the local area. ✘

I know it's true — I made it up myself...

Expert opinions, quotes and real-life examples show the reader you know what you're talking about. They'll also show the examiner that you know how to make a really persuasive argument. Sorted.

Think About Your Audience

Keep your reader's <u>point of view</u> in mind when you write, and grab yourself some juicy marks...

Put yourself in the **Reader's (or Listener's) Shoes**

1) Any piece of writing will be <u>read</u> or <u>heard</u> by someone — <u>match</u> your writing to your audience.

2) To do this, try to <u>guess</u> what your reader's reactions might be...

3) Your <u>first</u> paragraph is really important — make sure you've got your reader's <u>attention</u> right from the <u>beginning</u>.

4) Show you've thought about the reader's <u>point of view</u>.

Think about what the reader **Cares** about

Think about any <u>concerns</u> the reader might have, and then:

1) Make their concerns sound <u>reasonable</u>.

2) Let them know that you've <u>thought</u> about their concerns.

3) <u>Tell them</u> how your argument addresses their concerns.

A worry that people may have is the amount of litter after the concert. We will have a team working through the night to clear the area by the next morning.

Imagine how **People** may **Argue Against You**

A good way of persuading people is to imagine how they would argue <u>against you</u>, and answer their points. Imagine you're writing a letter to persuade the RSPCA to let you work for them...

First think up all the arguments <u>against</u> your opinion.

Reasons they wouldn't accept me
- too young
- lack of experience
- not enough time to spend
- what could I actually do to help?

Then you've got to work out how to <u>prove them wrong</u>.

- too young — but <u>parents say it's OK</u>
- lack of experience — but <u>want to learn</u> & <u>love animals</u>
- no time — can <u>arrange to do it</u> at weekends & after school
- what could I do? — <u>willing to do anything to help</u>

Me? Automatically disagree? Absolutely not...

Remember — if you can <u>think</u> like your readers, you'll always stay <u>one step ahead</u> of them.
If you can prove their <u>objections</u> wrong even before they've thought of them, you're onto a <u>winner</u>.

Persuasive Writing Tools

Writing a really <u>persuasive</u> argument can be hard work — here are some <u>more tips</u> to help you out.

Keep your writing *Polite*

1) Being polite is important when you're writing about people with the <u>opposite opinion</u> to yours.
2) You should criticise their <u>opinions</u> only — don't criticise them personally, or you'll sound angry.

> A lot of people think school uniforms make everyone equal. They are stupid and wrong...

> It is often said that school uniforms make everyone equal. This isn't true...

Talk *Directly* to your readers

Use '<u>you</u>' to talk <u>directly</u> to your readers, especially if you're trying to persuade them to do something.

For more on rhetorical questions, see p37.

Using 'you' makes the <u>reader</u> feel more <u>involved</u>.

> Giving blood saves lives. As a caring person, do <u>you</u> really need to read further before <u>you</u> take action?

This is a <u>rhetorical question</u>. The reader could only answer it in one way — to say 'no'.

Stories from *Real Life* can be *Entertaining*

1) Stories from real life can be a great way to persuade people by <u>entertaining</u> them — but keep them <u>short</u>.
2) You can make them up too, as long as they're <u>realistic</u>.

> Say you want to persuade parents to let their children cycle to school. Telling a <u>funny story</u> about when you were stuck in a really terrible traffic jam could persuade parents not to drive their kids to school.

> Stories can also be <u>more serious</u>. E.g. if you're persuading a local MP that the pavements in your street are dangerous, you could write about a time when your granny tripped and fell.

Use these techniques when you're writing to persuade...

Fantastic — <u>three ways</u> of making your writing punchy and persuasive. Use them wisely and they'll help to get the audience on your side, and help them <u>understand</u> the points you're making.

Writing to Inform, Explain or Advise

Non-fiction writing can <u>inform</u>, <u>explain</u> or <u>advise</u> — make sure you know what each one means.

Pick out the **Key Words** in the question

You need a clear idea of your <u>purpose</u> and your <u>audience</u>.
<u>Key words</u> in the question will tell you what the question's asking:

For more about leaflets, see p23.

> You are planning to open a shop in the town where you live.
> Write the text for a leaflet <u>informing</u> <u>local residents</u> about the shop.
> The leaflet should be about:
> * <u>where</u> the shop will be
> * <u>what</u> the shop will sell
> * <u>who</u> the shop is for

purpose

details to include

audience

Informing is about **Giving Information** *to your reader*

Writing to <u>inform</u> means <u>telling</u> your readers about a topic they may not know much about.

1) Informative writing can be <u>practical</u> — e.g. a leaflet giving information about Swine Flu.
2) Or it can be more <u>personal</u> — e.g. a writer informing readers about the time they ran the marathon.

> In either case, you should include plenty of clear <u>facts</u>.

Explaining means helping your readers to **Understand**

When you're explaining, you need to assume your readers <u>don't understand</u> the subject.

1) Give facts, examples and evidence.
2) Decide on the main points you want to make. <u>Explain</u> each point with an example or fact.
3) Tell your readers what any <u>technical terms</u> you use mean — see p.36.

Informing me about informing — too much information...

It's important to know the <u>difference</u> between informing and explaining. <u>Informing</u> is just giving your readers information. <u>Explaining</u> means helping people understand something they don't at first.

Writing to Inform, Explain or Advise

If you're <u>advising</u> someone, you have to sound like you <u>know</u> what you're talking about.

Advice needs to be based on the *Facts*

You might have to give <u>advice</u>, e.g. a letter to the council suggesting improvements to a sports centre.

1) Advice should <u>follow on</u> from information you've already written.

2) Keep your advice <u>formal</u> and <u>positive</u>. <u>Don't</u> write things like:

> "It's obvious that this should have been done years ago".

This sounds angry and negative

Written advice suggests what **Action** *to take*

1) When you're writing to advise, suggest to the reader what <u>courses of action</u> they could take.

2) You could give them different <u>options</u> so they have a <u>choice</u>.

3) Then it's up to the <u>reader</u> to take your advice... or not.

> You must tell someone if you're being bullied. This could be:
> • your parents
> • one of your teachers
> • your best friend

Plan *your writing carefully*

Think about the <u>main things</u> you want to say and note them down in a <u>plan</u>.

Here's an example of a "writing to inform" question:

> Write the text for an information leaflet about the sixth form at your school for potential students and their parents.

If the question includes bullet points, use these to plan your essay.

And here's a plan of the <u>main points</u> you might mention in your answer:

> <u>Purpose</u>: to inform   <u>Form</u>: leaflet   <u>Audience</u>: potential students and their parents.
>
> <u>Points to include</u>:
> 1) Big school — 1500 pupils.   2) Loads of choice of <u>subjects</u>.   3) Students get <u>good grades</u>.

Read the question, plan your answer, write it and check it...

Planning your writing is really <u>useful</u>. It'll help you answer the <u>question</u> and get lots of lovely <u>marks</u>. If you make a great plan, it'll also <u>stop</u> you from panicking in the middle of the exam. Excellent.

Writing to Inform, Explain or Advise

Always remember <u>why</u> you're writing your text — for more on <u>purpose</u>, see p.26.

Layout can help you Organise your writing

If you're writing a <u>leaflet</u>, you can use <u>headings</u> and <u>bullet points</u> to organise the text:

1) <u>Headings</u> break text up into <u>sections</u> and tell the reader what that section is <u>about</u>.
2) <u>Bullet points</u> are a good way to split information into lists of <u>facts</u>.

<u>Only</u> use these methods if it makes sense. E.g. headings work well in a newspaper article, bullet points work well in a leaflet. Otherwise, <u>write in paragraphs</u>.

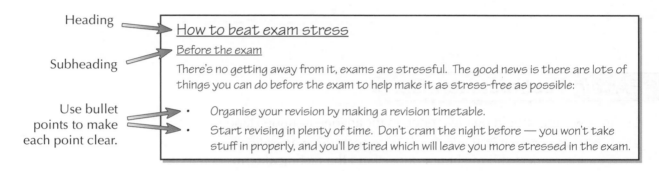

Heading

Subheading

Use bullet points to make each point clear.

<u>How to beat exam stress</u>

<u>Before the exam</u>

There's no getting away from it, exams are stressful. The good news is there are lots of things you can do before the exam to help make it as stress-free as possible:

* Organise your revision by making a revision timetable.
* Start revising in plenty of time. Don't cram the night before — you won't take stuff in properly, and you'll be tired which will leave you more stressed in the exam.

Using "I" or "You" can sound too personal

If you use "I..." a lot, it can sound as if you're just expressing <u>your opinion</u>.
That's fine for some pieces but it can make information or advice sound <u>unconvincing</u>.

<u>I have noticed</u> that the temperature of the swimming pool water has been rising for the last 3 months.

 This leaves room for doubt — did you just 'notice', or did you actually measure it?

The temperature of the swimming pool water has been rising over the last 3 months.

 Sounds like a statement of fact.

Using "I..." can be handy if you're writing about your <u>own</u> experience. Just don't use it all the time.

The structure of your writing is really important...

Using <u>headings</u> and <u>bullet points</u> can help to give your writing a really clear <u>structure</u>, but you should only use them if they're <u>suitable</u> for the form you've been asked to write in.

Make Sure Everyone Can Understand

You've got to make sure that <u>everyone</u> knows what you're on about.

Think about your **Readers**

If you're writing to <u>inform</u> or <u>explain</u>, don't assume your readers will know everything about the topic.

1) Explain things which might be obvious to you, but not to <u>other people</u>.

This is no good —

> Get a plant and grow it.

You need to explain what you mean —

> Buy some seeds from a garden centre. Dig a small hole and put the seeds in the hole. Water the area regularly.

2) Guess where the reader might get confused and make those bits especially <u>clear</u>.

Explain **Technical** terms...

1) Your writing should be clear enough for anyone to <u>understand</u>.
2) Take care even when you're explaining something as <u>ordinary</u> as cooking dinner — some readers still might not understand the technical terms you're using.

The underlined words are <u>technical terms</u>. They'll be understood by tennis fans...

> The <u>serve-volley</u> game of Williams dominated Davenport's <u>ground strokes</u>.

...but others may not understand, and get confused.

...but don't make your language **Too Simple**

1) If you don't use the right words, it might seem like you don't know what you're talking about....

> There are several different types of singer. Some singers sound really squeaky when they sing, and some singers don't.

This is all pretty obvious — it would be better if the writer had <u>named</u> and <u>explained</u> the different types of voice (soprano, baritone etc.).

2) ... and sometimes it might be <u>unclear</u> what you mean.

> I have spoken to <u>many people</u> and <u>many of them</u> are concerned about graffiti.

'Many' is vague — be <u>more specific</u> and explain <u>how many</u> people and <u>who</u> they are (students, parents etc.).

But it all made perfect sense to me...

<u>Technical jargon</u> can be really confusing for some readers so it's <u>important</u> to explain these words. <u>Imagine</u> that the examiner doesn't understand technical language and you have to <u>explain</u> it to him.

Useful Language for Non-Fiction Texts

Here are some <u>extra</u> tips to make your writing even more <u>amazing</u>. Read carefully and practise.

Use **Rhetorical Questions** to **Involve** your audience

1) A <u>rhetorical question</u> doesn't need an answer — the answer should be obvious from the text.

> Is this sort of thing acceptable in our society?

2) Ordinary questions can be effective too.
Letting readers come up with the answer themselves is a great way to make them <u>agree with you</u>.

> Can anyone tell me why road builders are <u>ruining the countryside</u>?

Use <u>emotional language</u> (like "ruining the countryside") to <u>emphasise</u> your feelings on the subject.

Use **Lists** of **Three**

It's one of the <u>easiest</u> and most useful tricks for <u>emphasising</u> your points.
Instead of just using one adjective in a sentence, use <u>three</u>.

> Making children sit more exams would be <u>stressful</u>, <u>time-consuming</u> and <u>unreasonable</u>.

This sounds <u>much better</u> than "More exams would be stressful and time-consuming".

Be **Careful** when you're using **Exaggeration**

1) Sometimes you can use an <u>exaggeration</u> in your writing to make your point sound <u>stronger</u>.

> These days, teachers have to wade through <u>tonnes</u> of paperwork every week.

Your readers will realise you don't literally mean tonnes. It just <u>stresses</u> that you're talking about <u>a lot</u> of paperwork.

2) Use exaggeration <u>carefully</u>. If it's not <u>obvious</u> to the reader that you're exaggerating, they might think you're just a bit confused.

This exaggeration is the best thing ever...

The techniques on this page can be very <u>powerful</u>, but if you use them too much your answer will sound too wordy and confusing. Get them into your answer, but use them <u>carefully</u> and don't overdo it.

Warm-Up Questions and Worked Exam Answer

Warm-Up Questions

1. Define 'emotional language' and give an example.

2. Which of these is the less interesting and less vivid description? Why?
   a) He wore a long, black overcoat that was ragged at the edges and fading in colour. His tattered hat was tilted to cover his eyes. As he loomed over me, I felt my heart in my mouth. I couldn't breathe.
   b) He wore an old coat and when he came near me, I was scared.

3. Which is more likely to persuade your reader — a balanced argument or a ranting one?

Worked Exam Answer

1. Places can seem different at different times of year. Choose a place and write a letter to a friend telling them what that place is like in winter and in summer.

Essay plan:

1) *Begin by describing the country lane in winter — concentrate on the feelings of cold.*

2) *Describe the harshness of the landscape and the wildlife struggling to survive.*

3) *Describe the country lane in summer — contrasting the beauty of the landscape with that of winter.*

4) *Describe the wildlife and all of nature coming to life again.*

Essay: *Written in the form of a letter*

Dear Sameer,

    I'm so glad you're coming to visit in summer. East Ibley in winter is horrible! I went for a walk along the lane today and the rain was <u>freezing, like little bits of glass hitting me</u>. *Describes touch* The leaves were a dull brown mush that squelched underfoot and clung to my boots. The poplar trees, usually so tall and leafy, were ruined by the winter's cold, and each branch was empty and barren.

Worked Exam Answer

Dramatic images

The undergrowth around the trees appeared dark and gloomy, <u>as if it held dark secrets</u>. The whole scene was grey, as if life had been sucked from it.

The clouds looked like monstrous faces, as if <u>nature was angry at the world</u>. The branches from a fallen tree, blown over the night before, were scattered across the lane like litter. The rain was forming muddy pools and filling potholes.

Suggests how the scene makes her feel

When I was out, I saw a bird struggling to fly, whilst the wind and rain battered its wings. It kept on fighting, probably in search of safety and shelter. It reminded me of that bird we saw at the beach last winter.

But when you visit, it will be lovely. The poplar trees will be leafy again, and swaying gently in the summer breeze. We'll wander along, clutching ice creams and smelling of sun cream. I can't wait!

Compares with the details of the lane in winter

The sun's rays will be warm and gentle, and the <u>sky will be a deep, deep blue</u> at that time of year. There are so many flowers here in summer: proud, tall foxgloves and delicate <u>red poppies and bright white daisies popping up amongst the lush green grass</u>. Maybe we'll see butterflies, with white wings, flitting around in the haze of heat. There will be birds singing to each other, and lots of new life everywhere. It will look so different from how it all looks now.

Lots of objects and colours to describe the scene

I hope you're looking forward to the visit as much as I am!

Love Beth

Exam Questions

1. Write a letter to a friend telling them about your most memorable birthday celebration.

2. Write a talk for your year assembly about some work experience that you've done recently.

3. Write an article for your school newspaper, persuading students to do a sponsored walk for charity.
    The article should include:
    • Some details about the walk and where it will be held
    • Reasons why people should take part in the walk
    • Which charity the walk is raising money for and why it is important.

4. Write a letter to the board of governors at your school arguing for or against free musical instrument lessons for all students.
    The letter should be about:
    • Whether you are for or against the lessons and why
    • What the good or bad effects of the lessons might be
    • Whether parents and students would support your argument.

Revision Summary

This section has covered the main forms of non-fiction texts you're likely to come across during your English course, but don't panic if you get something a bit different — the basic advice is still the same. Think about your readers and what you're trying to achieve. Just to make sure you've got the hang of it, here's a page load of questions to test your knowledge.

1) How should your style of writing be different in a formal and an informal letter?

2) Name two techniques you could use in a newspaper article to make it easier to read.

3) If you're writing a film review, why is it important to include some facts about the film itself?

4) What's the main difference between a speech and other types of non-fiction text?

5) Give three examples of audiences you might write for. Say whether you would write in a formal or informal way for each one.

6) What is meant by the 'purpose' of your writing?

7) Put these points of a plan for a persuasive answer into the correct order:
   Emotional argument, Introduction, Logical argument, Conclusion, Other points of view.

8) Why is it important to be logical in your thinking?

9) How can using emotion help your argument?

10) Why might the sentence "Everyone has the right to an education" help get the reader on your side?

11) Why is it important to support your argument with facts?

12) Which of these quotes would be appropriate in an essay on getting good grades, and why?
   a) "Exams changed my entire existence", said a stranger in the street.
   b) "Getting good GCSEs has helped me to achieve what I want in life", said Simon von Norbury, Head of Marketing, Beards and Brogues Ltd.

13) Do all the facts and opinions you use in non-fiction answers have to come from real sources?

14) Do you need to try to put yourself in the reader's shoes? Why?

15) Why should you address any concerns you think your reader might have about your argument?

16) Give one reason why you might include a story from real life in your writing.

17) What's the main difference between informing readers about something and explaining it to them?

18) Why should you explain any technical terms you use in your writing?

19) What is a rhetorical question and why are rhetorical questions effective?

Different Types of Creative Writing

These pages cover <u>types</u> of creative writing — <u>check</u> with your teacher which ones you're doing.

Scripts and Speeches are Spoken

1) Text for a <u>script</u> or <u>speech</u> (see p.44) can be written in the <u>voice</u> of a <u>specific person</u>, e.g. a character from a piece of fiction.

2) Think about what kind of <u>words</u> characters would use, whether they use <u>formal language</u> or a <u>dialect</u>.

3) If your script is for <u>more than one</u> person, give each person their own style.

This stuff will also come in useful for the 'Writing for the Spoken Voice' part of Edexcel English Language.

Articles and Reviews can Entertain

Think about the <u>audience</u> and <u>purpose</u> of the text, e.g.:

- an <u>article</u> in a magazine could be either <u>humorous</u> or <u>serious</u>.
- a film <u>review</u> should give an <u>opinion</u> — it shouldn't just describe what happens in the film.
- a newspaper article will be <u>serious</u> in style, but could include <u>quotes</u> and descriptions.

Descriptive Writing and Stories also Entertain

1) You might have to tell a <u>story</u> or <u>describe a scene</u> (see p.47-50).

2) You may be given the <u>title</u> or maybe the first or last <u>sentence</u> .

3) You might be asked to write from your <u>own</u> point of view, or from <u>someone else's</u> point of view.

Voice-overs explain Images

1) Voice-overs are the <u>scripts</u> that go with documentaries, TV adverts, etc (see p.44). They can be <u>informative</u>, like the example on p.44, or <u>persuasive</u>, like this:

> Scene: Slim, happy people playing frisbee on the beach
> Voice-over: Would you like to get fit, but don't have the time? Would you like to tone up, but can't afford expensive gym fees? Fallon's home gym could be the answer you're looking for...

2) If you're writing a <u>voice-over</u>, decide what images it will go with and <u>describe</u> them.

Everyone loves a story — especially about dogs and homework...

These are just some examples of creative writing, but there are loads more, e.g. leaflets, emails, blogs... Whatever you're writing, always think about <u>who</u> you're writing for and <u>why</u> you're writing.

Planning Your Writing

Planning is as important for creative writing as it is for any other kind of writing.

Structure your writing to suit the Purpose

1) Use a structure that suits what you want to achieve.
2) You won't get any marks for layout, only content.
3) Bear in mind how many words you're expected to write.
4) Make it really clear which bits are important. Add details and write varied sentences.
5) Write out a detailed plan.

For example, if you're planning a short story:

- Start with something unusual or exciting that will make your reader curious.
- As long as you have a plot worked out, you can use any order you like.
- Just be sure to keep it relevant. Make sure that every point is related to the story.

You could have a character running from something — this'll get your reader wondering why.

Your character could be very old at the start of the story, talk about events that happened when they were young.

Choose your writing Style to match your Audience

Work out who your audience is before you start writing, and think about what style you need to use:

Write a report for a local newspaper on the discovery of the bodies of Romeo and Juliet.

Keep the tone of your writing formal. Readers wouldn't expect a funny report about death.

If you're writing for a teenage audience, you can be more informal.

You've been asked to write a film review for a website aimed at teenagers.

If you're not told who the audience is, write for the examiner and keep it fairly formal.

Give your writing a clear structure to make it flow...

Your readers will notice if your writing doesn't make sense or is in a strange order.
Emphasise important points by going into detail and using different sentence styles.

Moving Images

Here's a great chance to <u>write</u> about <u>movies</u> and <u>TV shows</u>.

You might have to *Write* a *Film Review*

1) Provide <u>information</u> about the film — e.g. what it's about.
2) Think about <u>who you're writing for</u> and whether <u>they'd</u> enjoy the film.
3) Use <u>persuasive language</u> to <u>convince</u> people to see it.

List of three used to build excitement.

This sci-fi summer blockbuster is packed full of amazing <u>CGI</u>. <u>Galaxies explode, new worlds are discovered and alien forces fight</u>.

Specialist words related to films.

You could be writing a *Script* or a *Voice-over*

<u>Voice-overs</u> are read out by an unseen presenter to tell the viewer about the images on screen, e.g. in <u>adverts</u> and <u>documentaries</u>.

Show what viewers would see.

Scene: <u>Underwater, daytime, blind fish swimming</u>.
Voice-over: Isolated for generations in a network of caves beneath the Rio Grande, the Mexican Tetra has developed several unique adaptations to life in a world without light. These creatures <u>have no eyes and each one is pinkish-white</u>...

Give the voice-over person plenty of chances to take a breath.

Give lots of information.

You could write a *Short Story* for a *Film* to be *Based On*

You might have to write a <u>text</u> that will be <u>adapted</u> for a film or TV drama. Use <u>detailed descriptions</u> to tell the <u>director</u> about the <u>characters</u> and <u>settings</u>.

This gives loads of detail that the director could use.

<u>Late one misty Bristol evening in autumn 1879</u>, Dr Procktar headed to the quayside. <u>As always, he wore his trademark battered brown overcoat</u>. The frayed bullet hole in the left lapel was now a vivid reminder of how fortunate he had been <u>in Munich, just two months earlier</u>...

Describes the lead character to give the director clues.

Sets up a possible flashback and suggests more settings.

You need to use lots of detailed description...

Just remember, each type of writing needs a different mix of <u>facts</u>, <u>persuasive</u> writing and <u>description</u> to really impress the examiner. Trust me, it helps to think ahead and <u>plan</u> your work first.

Re-creations

You can turn <u>fiction texts</u> into <u>different types</u> of writing.

You might change a **Play** or **Poem** into a **Short Story**...

1) Turning something into a short story gives you the chance to add to the original text.

2) You could use the <u>speech</u>, <u>characters</u> and <u>stage directions</u> from plays, or the <u>feelings</u> and <u>themes</u> from a poem.

3) You could change it so it's written from the point of view of <u>one of the characters</u>.

4) Here's an example that changes a scene from <u>Macbeth</u> into a <u>short story</u>:

You could use actual lines from the play or change them.

Extra details add excitement.

> "<u>Why did you bring these daggers from the place?</u>" hissed Lady Macbeth, glaring at the sight of her husband's crimson hands, and making no effort to hide her impatience with him. <u>Macbeth's vacant gaze drifted from her stern brow to the weapon trembling in his palm as though trying to free itself from his twisted fingers</u>...

...or change a **Text** into **Non-Fiction Prose**

<u>Non-fiction prose</u> could mean things like <u>articles</u> or <u>radio broadcasts</u>.

For example the events in '<u>Of Mice and Men</u>' could be turned into a <u>newspaper article</u>:

The headline is appropriate for an article.

Details show you understand the original text.

> <u>LOCAL MAN AND WOMAN FOUND DEAD</u>
> Details are emerging, after two bodies were found near <u>Soledad</u> yesterday. The first, the body of a young female, was found in a barn in the late afternoon. Less than an hour after the discovery of the woman, a second fatality was reported in an area of woodland just <u>three quarters of a mile away</u>. <u>It is understood</u> that the deaths are both being treated as suspicious, and <u>are believed</u> to be linked in some way.

Crime reports usually include factual detail.

These phrases make it sound more formal.

There are lots of different ways to change your fiction text...

You might be asked to change a website into a blog, or an image into a film script, or a radio podcast into a diary entry. Just remember — think about the <u>features</u> of the different <u>types</u> of text.

Commissions

Having to write on a <u>specific theme</u> is a bit daunting — that's why planning is the key to success.

Some Themes have lots of *Different Meanings*

You might be asked to write on a theme that seems pretty vague.
It could be something with <u>more than one meaning</u> or a <u>broad</u> topic like this:

> Write a creative piece on the theme 'The Four Seasons'.

1) Scribble down all the things that <u>spring to mind</u> straight away.
2) Once you've jotted down all you can, <u>decide which idea</u> to write about.
3) Then think about the <u>purpose</u> of your text, what <u>form</u> it'll take and <u>who</u> you're writing it for.

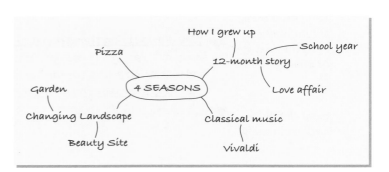

Other Themes can be more *Specific*

You might choose a task where you have to do a particular <u>type</u> of creative writing.
The <u>purpose</u>, <u>form</u> or <u>audience</u> may have <u>already</u> been decided for you.
Have a look at the questions <u>below</u> for an idea of the kinds of things you might get:

> Write a letter to the town council explaining a problem in the town and how it could be solved.

Purpose: inform/advise
Form: letter
Audience: councillors

> Write an article about one of your hobbies for your school or club website.

Purpose: inform (& persuade?)
Form: online article with lots of facts
Audience: school community / visitors

Don't just dive straight in and start writing...

Be smart. Pick a topic to suit your strengths and style — if possible, write about things you're <u>interested</u> in. And remember, if you want to get plenty of marks it helps to <u>plan</u> your answers.

Descriptive Writing

A <u>great</u> piece of descriptive writing will really bring a scene to <u>life</u> in the reader's mind.

You're painting a **Picture** with **Words**

1) When you're <u>writing to describe</u>, remember that the <u>reader</u> won't have the same <u>picture</u> in their head as you have in yours — you need to <u>draw it</u> for them with words.

2) Come up with <u>creative</u> ways to describe what you're thinking about.

3) You can use your <u>own experiences</u> — but remember you can add in <u>invented details</u> too.

Imagine you're making a **Film** of the scene

Imagine that you're making a <u>film</u> of your scene, and you're describing what will happen in it.

1) Think about how the scene will <u>look</u> at <u>different times</u> of the day, or in <u>different seasons</u>.

> *The beach was lonely and grey, empty of all movement except the soft splash of waves. It was hard to believe that it would soon be alive with tourists and brightly-coloured deck chairs.*

2) Or you could <u>zoom</u> in or out of your scene, <u>describing things</u> as you go.

> *I was only feet away from the last of the day's fishermen looking out to sea. The reflections of trees shimmered on the water, and in the distance I could just make out the hazy form of hills.*

Think about each of the **Senses** when you write

You can't use every single one all the time but the senses can be used to make a scene <u>come to life</u>.

Sight
How things looked...

The wall crumbled away to reveal a small tunnel winding into the distance.

Sound
How things sounded...

Sam heard a faint, dripping sound from inside the cave.

Smell
How things smelled...

As she walked on, a smell like rotting vegetables filled her nostrils.

Taste
How things tasted...

The soup tasted salty and contained lots of chewy lumps.

Touch
How things felt...

There was a sharp crunch under her foot. It felt like the shell of a snail cracking.

The reader needs to be able to imagine what you're writing about...

OK so all this 'paint a picture with words' stuff might sound weird, but it's the best way to get this right. Make sure you use a <u>broad range</u> of language and describe things using different <u>senses</u>.

Narrative Writing

Narrative writing is a chance to <u>write a story</u> — write about something you're <u>interested</u> in.

*Get your story straight **Before** you start writing*

Once you've got a rough idea of what you're going to write, jot down a brief <u>breakdown</u> of your story's plot.

1. **Beginning**   Start by <u>introducing</u> your key characters.   →   *A lot of stories are about conflict or a struggle. That's because characters have different motives which clash.*

2. **Build-up**   What's going to happen — how will you build up to the <u>climax</u> of your story?   →   *Give your characters a challenge. There has to be an element of risk to make it exciting.*

3. **Climax**   The main event or <u>turning point</u> should happen now.   →   *You need to build up the suspense and keep your reader guessing up until this point.*

4. **Ending**   Be sure that your <u>conclusion</u> makes some kind of point.   →   *You could give the story a moral, or end it with an unexpected twist.*

*Check that your story has **These Things***

1) Whatever was stated in the <u>question</u>, e.g. the first line.

2) An entertaining <u>plot</u> that says something.

3) A clear <u>structure</u> with a beginning, middle and end.

4) Different <u>sentence structures</u> and interesting <u>vocabulary</u>.

5) Realistic and entertaining <u>dialogue</u>.

6) Correct <u>paragraphs</u>, <u>punctuation</u> and <u>spelling</u>.

Learn the four plot stages of a good story...

Think of a story or film you like and jot down its <u>plot</u>. See if you can find the <u>four</u> plot stages.
Thinking about how other writers develop their plots will help you with your own writing.

Narrative Writing

Bring characters to <u>life</u> and make things more <u>interesting</u> by including lots of detail and emotions.

Write good *Descriptions* using *Images*

1) Give <u>specific details</u> that set the scene for the reader, and help emphasise the important points.

2) Use <u>inventive images</u> to get the reader to create a mental picture of what's happening.

Sam lived with her mum in Chorlton, Manchester.

This... ✗

Sam lived in Chorlton, Manchester with her mum. She spent most of her time in her tiny attic bedroom. It was a damp, musty place, and she often heard rats scuttling at night.

...is not as good as this. ✓

Write from your *Own Viewpoint* or from *Someone Else's*...

1) A good story <u>gets inside the characters' heads</u> and really thinks about their <u>thoughts</u> and <u>feelings</u>.

2) One way of doing this is to write from your <u>own viewpoint</u>. For example:

> I've always loved horse-riding, the thrill of the gallop, the sweet smell of hoof-crushed grass, the unspoken understanding as my horse and I move as one. But the bond between me and my horse, Cloud, was really tested one windswept evening in November.

3) Another good technique is to write the <u>character's thoughts</u> as if they were <u>speaking out loud</u>, e.g.:

> Emily stood by her window, getting ready to lower a basket of treats from her bedroom to children in the street below. "I must remember not to lean out too far," she thought to herself. "I don't want strangers to see me."

4) <u>Think</u> about <u>why</u> you (or the character) <u>feel</u> the way you do —
e.g. <u>don't</u> just start a story with "Erin was scared of dogs", explain <u>why</u> she was scared.

Make the *Important* parts really *Stand Out*

You have to make sure your reader really <u>understands</u> which bits are important.
Give <u>details</u> and try to <u>vary your style and vocabulary</u>.

<u>Think about why what you're describing matters:</u>
- Who cares about it?
- What effect does it have on your characters?
- How does it influence what happens in the plot?

Interesting characters make interesting stories...

Describing scenes and characters makes it really easy for the reader to <u>imagine</u> what's going on in your story. Try to describe <u>unusual</u> places or characters that the examiner will be really interested in.

Style and Finishing Your Narrative

Your writing will work better if you don't always write in exactly the same way.

Vary your Structure and Style

Changing the pace and style of your sentences and paragraphs will make your writing more interesting. You could change between long, descriptive sentences and shorter ones to match the mood of your story.

These sentences are short.
They sound slower.

> It was Ahab's turn to keep watch. All his shipmates were gently nodding off to sleep. Even the waves seemed to nod slowly as if in a trance. Out of nowhere a gigantic whale surfaced right by the boat, blowing out a thousand bubbles, and everyone woke up and shouted, clutching at the rails for safety.

This sentence is longer.
It speeds up, and sounds more energetic.

Short sentences don't always slow the pace down.
They can be short and punchy to describe action scenes.

> He saw me and yelled. I turned and ran. I was scared. I didn't see the step. I hit the deck. That's all I know.

Plan the Ending carefully

Spend a bit of time planning the conclusion (see p.48).

1) You could aim for the unexpected by finishing your story with a twist.
   Drop some hints earlier on in the plot, to refer back to.

2) Give your plot a moral so that the story proves a point.
   You could borrow a moral from a fairy tale.

3) You need a paragraph at the end of your story that ties up all the loose ends of the plot.

4) The last line is important — it should sum up the story for the reader and leave them satisfied.

Try to move the story on to keep the reader interested...

Vary the pace in your story to keep the reader interested — then they'll want to read all the way to the end. Don't ever, ever disappoint them and finish by saying you woke up and it was all a dream.

Getting Through the Assessment

You can't just wing a controlled assessment with no preparation. Make sure you're ready for it.

Double Check exactly what you have to do

You'll have to do at least one creative writing task as part of the controlled assessment.
Depending on your exam board, you might have to do some creative writing in an exam as well.

1) Check that you know how many tasks you have to do.
2) Know how long you have to complete each task and how many words you'll have to write.
   If there isn't a word limit, you'll be given some guidance on roughly how much to write.
3) Read the instructions carefully.

Do your Research and Preparation Carefully

1) Use your preparation time to work out the key points to include.

2) You can use the internet, books and other resources for your research.

3) When you're doing research, make loads of notes. Always write down
   where you got information from so you'll be able to find it again quickly.

4) When you've done your research write up neat copies of your notes to take into the assessment.
   You can't take a draft answer in with you but you can take in a short plan so make it clear and useful.

Check Your Grammar and Presentation at the end

1) Leave yourself enough time at the end of each task to read your work carefully.

   - Check that your writing is clear and readable.
   - Check your spelling. You won't have access to dictionaries
     or spell-checkers so double-check any difficult words.
   - Check your punctuation and grammar.

2) When the time's up make sure you've filled in your candidate details before you hand it in.

Plan your way to a great assessment...

And that's it — how to have a happy controlled assessment. Know exactly what you will have to do.
Do enough preparation so you can do it really well. Then walk in, sit down and you're ready.

Warm-Up Questions and Worked Exam Answer

These warm-up questions should ease you gently in and make sure you've got the basics straight. If there's anything you've forgotten, check up on the details before you go onto the worked exam answer and the exam questions.

Warm-Up Questions

1. An interesting or unusual beginning will grab your reader's interest. Which two of the following openings make you want to read on, and which ones are boring? Explain why.
   a) Ali had lived in Slough all his life. He lived with his parents and four sisters.
   b) The neighbours had always thought that there was something strange about Ali.
   c) Ali had black hair and brown eyes. He wore earphones.
   d) Ali had seen something terrible, and his life would be changed forever.

2. List the five human senses that can be used to make your story more realistic. Write a brief example sentence for each of the five senses that could be used in a story.

3. Write a paragraph that uses a combination of long and short sentences to change the pace of your writing.

4. Why is the very last line of your conclusion important?

Worked Exam Answer

1. Write about a journey that you have made, and that you enjoyed very much.

   Essay plan:
   1) *important info about the journey — where, who with, preparation, plans*
   2) *start of journey, feelings, observations of other people*
   3) *continuing to hotel, observations of other people*
   4) *arrival at hotel, waiting to begin climb before dawn, feelings*
   5) *conclusion — feelings at end of journey*

Mount Kinabalu

Good introduction giving information about the journey.

Last year my family and I 'climbed' Mount Kinabalu, the highest mountain in South East Asia. The journey took a day and a half, walking to a hotel by the first afternoon, and making the final climb before dawn. It was challenging but I enjoyed the sense of achievement.

 Repetition of wording from the question is good.

Worked Exam Answer

Range of emotions: 'enjoyed', 'worried', 'uncomfortable'.

Our journey began in the Kinabalu National Park, where we met our guide, Mario. I felt worried, and uncomfortable about having a stranger with us. I was quiet as we set off through the rainforest but, when Mario showed us insect-eating plants, I began to feel excited. Soon, the terrain changed from dark forest to steps cut from the mountainside. I felt tired because of the thin air as we climbed higher. We began to see the first groups of people coming down the mountain.

Change of feelings

Vivid description

We often stopped to sip water, nibble energy bars and to take photographs. By midday everyone was breathing heavily. The air had turned cold, and a silver mist was moving around us. We were now walking on grey rock. We were amazed to see three local women carrying large gas cylinders in baskets on their backs - supplies for the hotel!

Describing people and scenery makes it more interesting.

We reached the hotel by late afternoon. After a simple meal we tried to sleep, but we were too excited. In the morning, everyone was awake when Mario called us. We set off in the pitch-dark, our torches lighting up the white rope marking the way to the top.

The exclamation marks add to the excitement.

Good use of the senses: touch and sound.

Suddenly, I saw other torches. We had arrived! We had walked to the top of the highest mountain in South East Asia! I was very excited! The wind was icy and we heard it whistling round us so we pulled on hats and gloves.

This sentence rounds off the essay and refers back to the question.

Soon we began our descent, which took about four hours. I hardly remember the return journey. I had climbed the highest peak in South East Asia, and I was delighted!

Exam Questions

1. Describe an important event in your life, and say what effect the incident had on you.

2. Write about your first day at your present school.
    Explain how you felt at various times during the day.

3. Write a descriptive piece on the theme of winter.

4. Describe a time when you were very frightened.
    You may write about this in any way you like — a real or an imaginary situation.

Revision Summary

Loads of people get really worried over this original writing bit — but you just need to learn the tricks that make stories seem really interesting and clever.

So make sure you go through every single one of these questions and examples, and you'll see just how easy it can be.

1) What is a voice-over?
2) If you're not told who your audience is, what kind of style should you write in?
3) Why do you need to include plenty of pauses when writing scripts and voice-overs?
4) What different types of writing might you turn non-fiction texts into?
5) If you're writing a text that will be adapted for the screen, how can you help the director?
6) You have been commissioned to write creative pieces for the following themes.
   Jot down three ideas for:
   a) Hair
   b) Escape
   c) Moving Out
7) a) Give a short example of an <u>interesting</u> and a <u>boring</u> description of someone's face.
   b) Explain why one is better than the other.
8) Why might it be helpful to write about your own experiences?
9) Choose two of the five senses and give an example of how each might be used to describe a house in a short story.
10) For each of the following parts of a story, explain what each one should do:
    a) Beginning
    b) Build-up
    c) Climax
    d) Ending
11) True or false: You shouldn't think about a character's thoughts and feelings when writing a story?
12) Let's say you've just had a trip on a magic flying carpet.
    Write an interesting paragraph about your trip. Try to change the pace and style of your sentences throughout the paragraph.
13) What could you do to make sure your creative writing has a strong ending?
14) What kind of notes can you take in to your controlled assessment?
15) What should you check for once you've finished writing?

Writing about Prose, Drama and Poetry

There are different <u>types</u> of literature questions and <u>you</u> need to know how to answer <u>all</u> of them.

These are the **Different Types** of text you'll **Study**

Texts from the literary heritage

- Think about the society the novel is set in.
- If it's an extract, make sure you talk about language and give lots of examples.

Poetry

- If you studied a group of poems in class, you'll be asked questions about them.
- You might get one or two unseen poems to write about.

Modern prose or drama

- You'll be asked questions about a modern novel or play you studied in class.
- Think about characters, theme and language.

A Shakespeare play

- You'll get an extract from the play to analyse, or a question about characters or themes.
- Whatever the question, talk about the language Shakespeare uses.

Texts from different cultures

- You'll be asked about the whole text or an extract.
- Show you understand the social and historical background of the text.

Don't worry — you might not be studying all of these...

Here's how to tackle literature questions...

Step 1 — Work out **What The Question Is About**

1) The question's likely to be <u>about</u> one of <u>four</u> things:

- THEME — what the play, poem or story is about, e.g. love/conflict.
- SETTING — the importance of the place(s) where the text is set.
- CHARACTERISATION — how the writer puts across information about the characters.
- WRITER'S SKILLS — the techniques that the writer uses to influence the reader.

2) When you're writing about a text from a <u>different culture</u> or from the <u>literary heritage</u> you'll also have to write about the <u>time period</u> and <u>culture</u> (see p.65).

Choosing the right question is really important...

If you get a <u>choice</u> of questions, it'd make sense to pick one which gives you lots of <u>ideas</u> of stuff to write. Make sure you're answering on a text you've actually <u>studied</u> too...

Writing about Prose, Drama and Poetry

Now you've really got to grips with the <u>question</u>, follow these steps to write a great <u>answer</u>.

Step 2 — *Break* the question into **Bullet Points**

1) You <u>can't</u> give a one-sentence answer to literature questions.
You have to <u>use detail</u> and make lots of <u>separate points</u>.

We've just used 'Little Red Riding Hood' as an example — it won't be in the exam.

> Write about the ways in which Little Red Riding Hood is shown to change or stay the same in the course of the story.

2) The exam paper might help you by breaking the question down into <u>bullet points</u>.
If it doesn't, work out some of your own, like the ones below.

> Write about:
> * What she says and does
> * Her attitudes and feelings
> * How the writer shows you how she changes or stays the same.

Step 3 — *Now make a* **Plan**

Write a plan based on your own <u>bullet points</u> or the ones given.

* What she says and does.
  Beginning — picking flowers, no hurry to get to Grandma's
  End — she tricks the wolf

* Her attitudes and feelings.
  Beginning — feels confident and secure
  End — cross with herself, even more confident

* How the writer shows you how she changes or stays the same
  Beginning — 'drifted along,' compares her to a butterfly
  End — looks the wolf in the eye, 'now she knew what to do.'

You <u>don't</u> have to use full sentences in a plan, just get your ideas in <u>order</u>.

Show how she changes by <u>comparing</u> the beginning to the end of the story.

Use short <u>quotations</u> to back up your points.

When you're <u>planning</u>, <u>stick to the question</u>. Write about the <u>same</u> amount for each bullet point.

Make sure your plan actually answers the question...

<u>Breaking</u> the question down into <u>bullet points</u> is a really useful way of planning your exam answer.
Keep thinking about <u>what</u> the question is asking when you're planning to get lots of marks.

Writing about Prose, Drama and Poetry

Once you've <u>written</u> your plan, make sure you <u>stick</u> to it when you write your answer.

Step 4 — Write a brief **Introduction** then follow the plan

Your introduction should be <u>pretty short</u> — a quick answer to the question.

> There are several events in the story which show how Little Red Riding Hood changes, such as the escape from her Grandmother's house. They show how she starts off trusting, but learns from her experience.

The rest of your essay should <u>back up</u> your introduction.

> 1) Deal with the <u>bullet points</u> in order.
> 2) <u>Don't</u> keep switching between different ideas. Deal with <u>one</u> idea at a time in <u>separate paragraphs</u>.

For more on writing in paragraphs, see p.5-6.

Step 5 — Talk about your **Personal Response**

1) You need to talk about your <u>personal response</u> to the text — what you think the author's trying to say and how they're trying to make the reader <u>feel</u>.
2) There are lots of <u>different ways</u> of interpreting a text — use quotes to back up <u>your</u> interpretation.
3) Your <u>response</u> needs to fit the question. If it's 'How does the writer present the character of Little Red Riding Hood?' say 'The reader <u>feels surprised</u> that such an innocent young girl manages to outsmart the wolf in the end.'

Step 6 — Don't forget the **Conclusion**

1) Always leave enough <u>time</u> to write a proper conclusion.
2) Make sure you've <u>answered</u> the question.
3) Sum up with your <u>main idea</u> again — but say it differently.

Your conclusion is the last thing the examiner will read — don't rush it.

> At the start of the story Little Red Riding Hood doesn't have a care in the world. By the end she has been through a terrifying experience. The writer shows that she has learnt from her experience and become more cautious.

Spend a few minutes planning — but don't waste time...

When you're practising exam answers, <u>time</u> yourself even when you're <u>planning</u> your essay. There's no point in spending <u>forever</u> planning an answer and then not having <u>time</u> to write anything...

Writing about Characters

You might need to write about the way the author <u>creates</u> their characters.

Characters are always there for a *Reason*

1) When you're answering a question about a <u>character</u> in a poem, play or novel, don't talk about them as if they're real people — make it clear that the author has <u>created</u> them to get a message across.

2) A character's <u>appearance</u>, <u>actions</u> and <u>language</u> all help with this.

3) Find descriptions of how they <u>look</u> or what they <u>do</u>, then think about what this might say about them.

Lord of the Flies — William Golding

Golding's description of Jack's face as "crumpled" and "ugly without silliness" makes us think that he might be an unpleasant person.

Of Mice And Men — John Steinbeck

The description of Lennie hurting the puppies when he strokes them tells the reader that he isn't in control of his own strength.

Work out the reasons *Why Characters Do Things*

1) Some characters are <u>motivated</u> by stuff like...

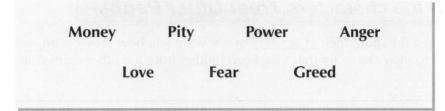

Money	**Pity**	**Power**	**Anger**
	Love	**Fear**	**Greed**

2) Some characters want things so badly that they <u>use</u> other people.

3) Some characters want to be <u>liked</u>, others want <u>revenge</u> or to feel <u>powerful</u>.

Animal Farm — George Orwell

Napoleon is motivated by a desire for power. He has "a reputation for getting his own way", and gradually becomes more powerful until he has total control over the animals.

Characters aren't real people — the author has designed them...

Remember, the author has <u>made</u> the characters exactly how he wants them. Your job is to work out <u>why</u> they're like that. Think about what would <u>change</u> if they were different, or if they weren't there.

Writing about Characters

Authors will leave <u>clues</u> in the text so you can tell what the <u>characters</u> are like.

Look at the way characters **Speak**

1) The way characters, including the narrator, <u>speak</u> tells you a lot about them.
2) The author <u>makes</u> them speak the way they do so you see them in a <u>particular way</u>.

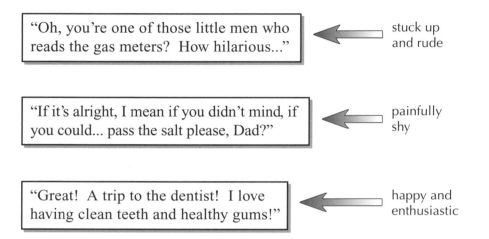

"Oh, you're one of those little men who reads the gas meters? How hilarious..." → stuck up and rude

"If it's alright, I mean if you didn't mind, if you could... pass the salt please, Dad?" → painfully shy

"Great! A trip to the dentist! I love having clean teeth and healthy gums!" → happy and enthusiastic

Look at how the characters **Treat Other People**

The writer tells you a lot about their <u>characters</u> by showing you how they get on with <u>others</u>. It can reveal sides to their character that they keep <u>hidden</u> from the other main characters.

Everyone loved Jack and thought he was warm and caring. But when a homeless man shuffled up and asked him for change, Jack spat into the man's face, saying "Don't ever speak to me again old man, or you'll be sorry."

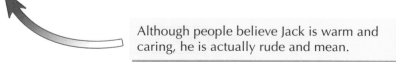

Although people believe Jack is warm and caring, he is actually rude and mean.

So, if you're writing about a <u>character</u>, don't forget to talk about their <u>relationships</u> with other <u>characters</u>. It will tell you a lot about what <u>kind</u> of person they are.

There's a reason for everything a character says or does...

The writer will make their characters talk in a certain way to give you <u>clues</u> about what they're like. Before the exam, read through your texts and make notes on each <u>major character</u> in the story.

Writing about Characters

This stuff should be going through your head whenever you've got a question about a character.

Stories can **Tell You** what characters **Think**

1) Novels and short stories might give <u>descriptions</u> of a character's thoughts and behaviour — the voice telling the story fills you in on <u>what characters are thinking</u>.

2) Pinpoint those bits, quote them, and say how they help answer the question.

> Sarah was disgusted by Jamie's behaviour at the bar and refused to speak to him.

> Sarah's reaction might make the reader think about Jamie in the same way.

3) Sometimes the reader might have a very different view of someone from the other characters, and this is good to talk about too.

> Jamie clenched his fists in frustration as he watched Sarah walk away. Everything he said or did came out wrong. He just wanted to be liked.

> Sarah is disgusted at Jamie, but the reader sees that he's misunderstood.

The **Narrator** is the person **Telling** the **Story**

There are two main types of narrator:

> 1) Third Person   2) First Person (see p.62)

A third person narrator tells you what's happening from outside the story, as if they were watching it happen. Books with a <u>third person</u> narrator can let you in on the secret thoughts of <u>all</u> the characters.

> Tamasine didn't want to tell anyone that she was ill. Of all her friends, no one suspected except Caitlin, and Caitlin didn't feel comfortable talking to anyone about it.

> The third person narrator reveals that Caitlin suspects Tamasine is sick. If we read the story from Tamasine's view we might not know that Caitlin suspects, or that she was uncomfortable about it.

Think about whether the author uses a first or third person narrator

Remember that the writer is responsible for everything you think about a particular character. Try to spot the tricks the writer's used to make you feel that way — that'll give you some good stuff to write about.

Writing about Characters

Sometimes the author doesn't speak to you directly. The characters do the talking for them.

The story can be Told by one of the Characters

When the story is told by one of the characters it's called <u>first person narration</u>.

1) First person narration gives you a first hand description of what the character <u>sees</u>, <u>says</u>, and <u>thinks</u>.

2) Sometimes the characters will <u>tell you</u> what they're like up front.

> I'm a complicated guy. I like to play mind games to try and confuse people. It gives me an advantage over them.

The narrator thinks he is clever and likes to be in control.

3) Sometimes characters <u>give something away</u> by their attitudes.

> That evening I went to a dinner party. If there's one thing I can't stand it's a group of people enjoying themselves. It makes me sick.

The narrator is unfriendly, and doesn't like being sociable.

First Person narrators can be Unreliable

First person narrators can't always be <u>trusted</u> because you're only getting <u>one side</u> of the story.

> All the other people there were boring fools. No one had anything interesting to say to me.

The narrator feels that he is better than the other guests. He might be, or he could just be very arrogant.

> The break-up was all her fault. She spent all her time with friends and she never trusted me.

The narrator doesn't want to take responsibility for the break-up. He could be blameless, or he might just be bitter about what happened.

You can't always trust a narrator — they're still a character...

Remember that the <u>narrator</u> has been created in a particular way by the author — think about <u>why</u>. Also, don't forget that first person narrators only give <u>one side</u> of the story — their own.

The Writer's Ideas, Attitudes and Feelings

<u>All</u> authors have <u>something to say</u>. All you need to do is write about what that is...

Message *questions can be hard to spot*

1) Questions about the message come in lots of <u>different forms</u>:

When the Woodcutter kills the Wolf what is the writer trying to show?	How does the author present ideas about hunger in the novel?	Why do you think the Woodcutter is important?

2) They're all asking about the story's <u>message</u>:

What does the writer think? Write about all the bits of the text that give it away.

Work Out the *Message* of your set texts *Before the Exams*

Make notes on the following things. I've done 'Of Mice and Men' as an example.

STORY

George and Lennie are friends who go to work at a ranch but dream of owning their own farm. Lennie keeps doing things wrong and other people don't understand him. This leads to his death.

CHARACTERS

Their relationships with each other cause problems for many of the characters.
The happiest characters in the book are the ones like Slim, who avoid close relationships.

TONE

Most characters dream about having a better life, as life on the ranch is sad and lonely.

TITLE

The title refers to a poem by Robert Burns. It means that even well thought-out plans can go wrong.

Once you've done that, <u>put it all together</u> to work out what the message is. I'd say it's something like...

The American Dream of a better, happier life is unrealistic but people still cling to it.

Write notes about the writer's message...

The writer's <u>message</u> could be pretty much anything. Making <u>notes</u> like the ones I've done above for 'Of Mice and Men' gives you all the <u>evidence</u> you need to back up the points you make in your essay.

The Writer's Techniques

The examiner loves it if you mention the writer's <u>style</u>. Here are some <u>tips</u> to help.

Writing Style affects the way you *Feel*

The <u>style</u> of a text is a combination of features like these:

words you hear every day	short, simple sentences	lots of fancy comparisons	lots of action

unusual, difficult words	long, complicated sentences	no fancy comparisons	lots of description

Show the examiners you understand how the writer's <u>voice</u> affects you.
E.g. If you're saying a character is <u>on the verge of insanity</u>, show how the style backs it up:

The writer makes the character speak in a very confused way. ⟹

> MAC: I'm late - late - late, better late than never Mother said to
>   me. I'm never late - never been better. So late, so late...

Pay attention to *Settings*

Writers use <u>settings</u> to affect how you feel. You could get a question asking how a <u>setting</u> from the text is used to create <u>atmosphere</u>. Look at how the writer makes the castle appear differently in these examples:

> The candlelight cast huge shifting shadows on the mossy walls. The wind howled down the chimney, throwing sparks around the room.

← This sounds creepy.

> The candlelight cast soft shadows around the room. I stretched out lazily in the armchair by the fire.

← This sounds a bit more enjoyable.

Look at the *Order of Events*

1) Stories aren't always told <u>in order</u>. Writers mess around with the order to keep you interested.
2) <u>Flashbacks</u> are where the scene shifts from the <u>present</u> to an event in the <u>past</u>.
3) <u>Foreshadowing</u> is where we're given clues about what will happen <u>later</u> in the story.

At the start of <u>Macbeth</u> the Witches predict what will happen to Macbeth.		Everything they predict comes true — though not always in the way Macbeth expects.

There's a lot to think about, but you can do it before the exam...

A writer's <u>individual writing style</u> is called their <u>voice</u>. It affects how the reader feels about characters, ideas and events. If you talk about it in your essay using these tips, the examiner will be <u>thrilled</u>.

Different Cultures

'Different Cultures' questions <u>aren't that different</u> from any others. Just look out for these things:

Talk about **How** the stories are **Written**

Write about the <u>same stuff</u> as you would in any literature essay, but look out for these things too:

1) <u>Unfamiliar words</u> from other languages or dialects (words used by people in a certain area).

> scuppernong   shinny   drew a bead

2) Words <u>spelt</u> so they sound like an accent or dialect.

> purty   fatta the lan'   settin'

Look at the author's **Thoughts and Feelings**

Think about what the writer wants to <u>say</u>, and write about their <u>values</u>, <u>ideas</u> and <u>attitudes</u>.

Feelings about <u>differences between cultures</u> come up all the time. E.g. a text might be about someone who's moved to a different country <u>feeling out of place</u>. Go into <u>detail</u> and <u>be specific</u>.

Don't just say:

> She is unhappy because she misses speaking her own language.

Say:

> English is not the poet's mother tongue. Speaking English all the time makes her feel damaged.

Much better — shows you understand <u>why</u> she's unhappy, and exactly how she feels.

It pays to **Know About** the writers

Try using the <u>internet</u> to find out about the <u>author</u> you've studied. You won't need to write loads about it, but it might help you come up with some new ideas.

1) Where the writer's from.
2) Information about their experiences.
3) How the poem or story fits in with the writer's life.

> John Steinbeck, <u>Of Mice And Men</u>
> 1) Born in California in 1902.
> 2) Spent time working on ranches when he was young.
> 3) Lived through the Great Depression and saw its effects.

Remember to back up the points you make with evidence...

Even if the question asks <u>mainly</u> about the way things are written, <u>don't</u> ignore the thoughts and feelings. The same goes for a thoughts and feelings question — <u>don't</u> ignore the way it's written.

Useful Literature Words

These words may <u>look</u> complicated but they're worth learning — they'll really <u>impress</u> the examiner.

Try to **Use These Words**

These words are very useful. Learn what they <u>mean</u> and how to spell them.

Don't get these two mixed up. simile	A simile <u>compares</u> one thing to another. Similes use the words 'like' or 'as'.	
	His socks stank <u>like a dead dog</u>.	His dog was as mean <u>as an old bandito</u>.
metaphor	Metaphors describe <u>one thing</u> as if it were <u>another</u>. Metaphors <u>never</u> use 'like' or 'as'.	
	My car <u>is a heap of old rubbish</u>.	My boyfriend <u>is a Greek God</u>.
imagery	This just means using <u>words</u> to <u>build a picture</u> in the reader's mind. Writers often do it by using <u>metaphors</u> and <u>similes</u>.	

a symbol	Where an object <u>stands for</u> an emotion or idea. Harry's pigeons flew high above the dismal suburban gardens. If Harry wanted to leave home, the pigeons could be a <u>symbol</u> of freedom.
emotive language	Language that makes you <u>feel</u> a certain way, e.g. sad or angry. Mean-faced Robbie stole the purse from Shelley's kind and cuddly grandma.
personification	When an object, or something in nature, is given <u>human characteristics</u>. The washing line sighed wearily under the weight of the laundry.

ambiguity	Words or events can have <u>more than one</u> possible meaning. If you notice something that could mean two or three different things then say so — it'll get you marks.
irony	The words say <u>one thing</u>, but the writer means <u>something else</u>. Say Carter is awful at football and has played badly in a game. The author writes: Carter really excelled himself this time. He's being ironic — he actually means 'Carter played even worse than usual.'

Cover the definitions and see if you can write them out again...

If you <u>forget</u> one of these words in the exam, <u>don't</u> panic. If you can see a writer's used a clever technique but you're not sure what to call it, then just <u>describe it in your own words</u>.

SECTION FIVE — WRITING ABOUT PROSE, DRAMA AND POETRY

Comparing

The <u>examples</u> on this page are about poems, but you could be asked to compare <u>any</u> of your texts.

Comparing = finding Similarities and Differences

Comparing means looking at two or more things <u>together</u>, and describing their <u>similarities</u> and <u>differences</u>.

> Compare these two poems. You should consider:
> * the language used
> * the ideas they contain
> * how the poems are presented

Make sure you spend an equal amount of time on each point in the question.

Compare both texts in Every Paragraph

Write about both texts <u>together</u> — <u>make links</u> between them. Tackle each point in the question in turn.

① — Whether the language used in the poems is similar or different.

→ In 'The Charge of the Light Brigade' Tennyson describes war using violent language, such as "Sabring the gunners." In contrast, Owen uses peaceful language like "whispering of fields half-sown" to describe the silence of the battlefield after the fighting.

② — The ideas they contain, and whether they're similar or different.

→ The soldier in 'Futility' has no name, which shows us that he has lost his individuality in battle. Similarly, in 'The Charge of the Light Brigade' Tennyson refers to the six hundred men as a group, so his soldiers don't have separate identities either.

③ — How the poems are presented, e.g. whether they're structured in the same way or not.

→ In 'Futility' both stanzas start with a command, which involves the reader in the poem. In 'Charge of the Light Brigade,' Tennyson involves the reader by using lots of repetition to remind them about how awful the battle was for the soldiers.

Practise comparing your texts when you're revising...

You could also be asked to <u>compare</u> the characters, messages, settings, structure or use of imagery in two texts. Make sure you think about these things <u>before</u> the exam and you're sorted.

Revision Summary

Section Five was quite a long one so have a go at these questions to see how much you've taken in. If you get stuck, have a look through the section and then try the question again. Keep doing this until you get them all right — you'll only be ready to move on to the next section when you can do that.

1) What must you make sure you cover in your plan?

2) What should you put in the introduction to your answer:
   a) At least eight good points
   b) The dog's dinner
   c) A brief answer to the question?

3) How many ideas should you cover in each paragraph of your essay?

4) What does 'personal response' mean?

5) What should you aim to do in your conclusion?

6) Which two of these are not ways in which characters help to get the writer's message across?
   a) The reasons why they do things
   b) The size of their feet
   c) Standing in the street holding a big sign
   d) The way they speak

7) Write down at least three things that could motivate a character.

8) Why might an author choose to use a narrator who is not a character in the text?

9) When a text is narrated by one of the characters why can't you trust what they say?

10) Think of one of the texts you've been studying in English lessons.
    Try to sum up the message of the text in one sentence.

11) List any three features of writing style.

12) Describe how you think the writer wants to make you feel in this paragraph:
    The curtain snapped in a sudden gust of wind. Outside an owl screeched.
    She put her hand to her ear and listened. Somewhere a tap was dripping
    and one by one the candles blew out.

13) What are flashbacks?
    a) The parts where the scene shifts to an earlier time.
    b) The bits that don't make any sense.
    c) The things they use to put streaks in your hair.

14) Which two of these are things you should write about when answering a question on a text from a different culture?
    a) How the stories are written.
    b) Your Nan's holiday to Majorca.
    c) Everything you know about the culture in the text.
    d) The author's thoughts and feelings.

15) Write a short explanation of what each of these technical terms means:
    a) simile   b) metaphor   c) imagery   d) irony

16) When you're comparing texts, what two aspects of them should you compare?

What You Have To Do

Basically, you need to be able to show that you've <u>understood</u> the play and the <u>way</u> it's been written.

Show you've **Understood** the play

1) Show that you understand <u>the order</u> everything happens in so you don't make silly errors.
2) You'll also need to show that you're familiar with <u>all</u> the characters, even the minor ones.
3) You need to <u>quote</u> little bits of text to back up your points and prove you've understood the play.

> You've got to know stuff <u>about</u> the characters — what they're like, how they behave, etc...

Explain the **Major Issues** the play deals with

Plays are about more than just the plot. Look out for these things in any play:

1) Social Issues   'An Inspector Calls' deals with the problems between social classes.

2) Moral Issues   'The Crucible' deals with justice.

Show you understand the **Significance** of the play

Almost all plays say something about <u>society and beliefs</u> at the time they were written, e.g.:

<u>WAR</u>	<u>JUSTICE</u>	<u>ORDER</u>	<u>LOVE</u>	<u>FATE</u>
What's the point? Is it a good thing?	What makes a good ruler? Can a ruler be fair?	Is freedom more important than law and order?	What is love? Is it always a good thing?	Do we control our own lives?

Come up with some **Ideas** of your own

1) Try to come up with something <u>original</u> — just make sure you back it up with a <u>quote</u> from the text.
2) Talk about your <u>personal response</u> — what <u>effect</u> the text had on you (did it make you <u>laugh</u>, <u>cry</u> etc.?).

Make sure you know what happens in the play and when...

It's a really good idea to know the <u>order</u> of events in the play you've studied. When you're revising, try scribbling down a <u>timeline</u> showing when the <u>important</u> things happen in the play. Then learn it.

What You Have To Do

When an author writes a <u>play</u>, they'll be thinking about the <u>effect</u> it will have, so you should too.

Write about the **Style**

1) Say what <u>effects</u> the playwright creates, e.g. suspense, humour, anger...

2) Mention any <u>imagery</u> — there's plenty of it in drama.

3) Try to spot how the words affect the <u>rhythm</u> —
   Short sentences can make a character sound excited. Longer sentences slow down the pace.

4) Look out for <u>repetition</u> — anything that's repeated is important.

Look out for any other language techniques — like the ones on p.64.

Show you know that plays should be **Watched** not **Read**

Show that you realise plays are meant to be <u>performed</u> by thinking about how effective they would look on stage and how an audience would react to them.

You can do this by throwing in the odd line a bit like this —

> This would look particularly spectacular when performed on stage because of the...

> This is a visual joke that an audience would find very amusing because...

Make sure you **Read** the **Stage Directions**

- As well as what the actors say, playwrights use things like <u>silences</u>, <u>actions</u> and <u>sound effects</u> to set a mood or to give the audience information.
- These things are often mentioned in <u>stage directions</u> (see page 71). Look out for them when you're writing about a scene, and say what <u>effect</u> you think they would have on the audience.

Plays are meant to be performed, not read...

You're not really supposed to <u>read</u> a play silently in your head — you're supposed to <u>act</u> it out. Think about how scenes in the play would look to the <u>audience</u> and how the action will <u>affect</u> them.

Reading Plays

You need to know how plays are <u>different</u> from novels and poems.

*Plays can be **Serious** or **Funny***

Tragedy

1) Tragedy is about <u>big topics</u> — e.g. religion, love, death, war.
   It usually involves the <u>downfall</u> of the main character.

2) Tragedies are really serious and moving. They often have a moral message.

Don't forget History Plays — they're any kind of play based on real historical events.

Comedy

1) Comedies are supposed to make you <u>laugh</u>.

2) Events and characters are based on things that happen <u>in real life</u>, but are much more silly and exaggerated.

Dialogue** is one character talking to **Another

1) If two or more people talk to <u>each other</u> it's called <u>dialogue</u>.

2) If one person speaks for a <u>long time</u> (to the audience and/or other characters) it's called a <u>monologue</u>.

> LORD CRUMB: Where exactly is the pizza?
> VERNON: In the basement, my lord.

3) A <u>soliloquy</u> is when a character speaks their <u>thoughts</u> out loud.
   <u>Only the audience</u> can hear what they're saying — other characters <u>can't hear a thing</u>.

***Stage Directions** describe the action on stage*

Write about <u>stage directions</u> — they tell you a lot about how the playwright wanted the play to look.

STAGE DESIGNS
scenery, lighting, special effects

> *A cluttered attic room: stuffed bear, upright piano.*
> *Moonlight filters through a dirty window.*

The room doesn't sound very well looked after.

ACTION

> *Unseen by Lord Crumb, Vernon slides the pizza into*
> *an envelope and conceals it beneath a cushion.*

Plays are different from novels and poems...

There are lots of special words about <u>plays</u> on this page — you'll <u>need</u> to learn them for your exam.
Write each one on a separate piece of paper, <u>shut</u> this book, then scribble a <u>definition</u>. Then check it.

Language in Shakespeare Texts

Shakespeare's plays are about 400 years old, so the language sounds weird to us.
It can seem daunting — but it all boils down to looking at who says what.

Be Specific when you write about Language

Think about what effect these things would have on the audience:

1) Imagery — look out for similes, metaphors and personification (see p.66).

> E.g., in 'Macbeth', images of darkness are used to symbolise Duncan's murder.

2) Striking words and phrases — these are words that jump out at you.

> E.g., in 'Romeo and Juliet', Tybalt says "Drawn, and talk of peace! I hate the word, as I hate hell, all Montagues, and thee". This shows us how angry he is.

3) Humour — look out for puns (words with double meanings) and jokes, and say what they show about the characters.

> E.g., As Mercutio dies in 'Romeo and Juliet', he says "Ask for me tomorrow and you shall find me a grave man." The pun on the word "grave" shows that Mercutio uses humour even in the most serious situations.

Look out for switches between Verse and Prose

Shakespeare's characters speak in a mixture of poetry and prose.

1) Most lines are written in blank verse. This has a regular rhythm but it doesn't rhyme.
2) It's grander than prose, but any character can use it.

> If music be the food of love, play on;
> Give me excess of it, that, surfeiting,
> The appetite may sicken, and so die.
> *Twelfth Night* Act 1 Scene 1

1) Rhyming verse is used at the beginning and ends of scenes or bits where a posh character is speaking or where a character is in love.
2) It makes the speech sound dramatic and impressive.

> Alas, that love, whose view is muffled still,
> Should, without eyes, see pathways to his will!
> *Romeo and Juliet* Act 1 Scene 1

1) The rest is written in prose.
2) Prose is mainly used for minor characters and funny bits.

> FESTE: Like a drowned man, a fool and a mad man: one draught above heat makes him a fool;
> *Twelfth Night* Act 1 Scene 5

Be aware of things Shakespeare's audience would have found funny...

The humour in Shakespeare plays is a bit different to now — audiences thought the idea of girls dressing up as boys was funny, so there are lots of jokes about that. As ever, use quotes to back up your points.

Warm-Up Questions and Worked Exam Answer

These warm-up questions should ease you in gently and make sure you've got the basics straight.
If you've forgotten anything, have another look at Section Six before you read the worked exam answer.

Warm-Up Questions

1. What should you do in your essays to prove to the examiner that you know the play?
   Write down all the 'true' options:
   a) get the facts straight about the story
   b) only write about the main characters
   c) quote whole scenes off by heart
   d) quote relevant snippets to back up each point you make.

2. Which of these sentences would show the examiner that you're thinking
   about the play being performed, not just read? Explain why.
   a) In this scene the language fills the audience with tension.
   b) In this scene the language is very tense.

3. Write a definition for each of the following words:
   a) stage direction
   b) tragedy
   c) dialogue
   d) soliloquy

4. In a Shakespeare play, what's the difference between poetic verse and blank verse?

Worked Exam Answer

1. Which members of the Birling family accept responsibility for Eva Smith's death
   at the end of 'An Inspector Calls'? Explain your answer.

Essay plan:

Keep the introduction short.

1) introduce the argument — some characters accept responsibility, others don't

2) show which characters haven't accepted responsibility and explain why

3) show which characters have accepted responsibility and explain why

4) conclusion — only Eric and Sheila accept responsibility

Important to show you've kept the question in mind.

Refer back to the question in the introduction.

Just before he leaves at the end of Act Three, the Inspector warns the Birlings to <u>accept responsibility</u> for others or face the consequences. However, <u>not all of the characters learn the Inspector's lesson by the end of the play</u>.

Sum up your argument in the introduction.

The older Birlings fail to accept responsibility for what has happened. <u>Mr. Birling</u> is a typical <u>Edwardian</u> self-made businessman who believes his only responsibility is to make money. He says that he had 'every excuse' for sacking Eva, and refuses to admit playing any part in

Mention the play's social / historical setting.

Worked Exam Answer

her death. When he thinks the enquiry was 'a piece of bluff', he's relieved because it will save his family from scandal, not because he feels guilty.

A paragraph for each character the question asks about.

Mrs Birling also cannot see her part in Eva's death, and is proud that she was 'the only one' not to give in to the Inspector. She is quick to blame others, particularly Eva, who she accuses of telling a 'pack of lies', and the father of Eva's child, who she says 'should be made an example of'. This is before she realises that the father is Eric.

Like Mr and Mrs Birling, Gerald denies responsibility and is very keen to present the case for the Inspector being a fake. He is the one who feels that 'everything's all right, now'. The older characters are 'amused' when they realise the Inspector was a fake, and quickly forget the effect that their actions could have caused. The same is true of Gerald, even though he is younger than Mr and Mrs Birling and not part of their family.

Show how the characters change — say what they were like before.

The character who seems to feel the most responsibility for Eva's death, and who is most changed by it, is Sheila. She is first presented as being vain and spoilt, as is shown by the Milward's incident. She recognises the Inspector's intentions very early on, saying 'you talk as if we were responsible', and she quickly realises that they are. Not only does she accept responsibility for her own actions, even when everyone else believes that the enquiry was a hoax, she also tries to make the others see how serious their actions were, saying 'You began to learn something. And now you've stopped.'

Use quotes to back up your argument.

Similarly, Eric changes from being immature to becoming aware of the consequences of his actions. The audience sees this when Gerald suggests there may have been 'four or five' girls involved in the events described by the Inspector, and Eric replies, 'that doesn't matter to me. The one I knew is dead'.

Summarise your arguments in the conclusion and refer back to the question.

Only the younger members of the Birling family, Eric and Sheila, accept any responsibility at the end of the play. As the Inspector says, the 'young ones' are 'more impressionable'.

Finishing with an appropriate quote is a nice touch.

Exam Questions

<u>You are allowed to use the text to write your essay.</u>

1. How far is Friar Lawrence responsible for the deaths of *Romeo and Juliet*?
    You may wish to think about:
    - The events leading up to the deaths of Romeo and Juliet
    - How Friar Lawrence could be responsible for the deaths
    - Who else could be responsible for the deaths

2. How does Shakespeare present the character of Macbeth as both good and evil?
    You may wish to think about:
    - How Macbeth behaves at the beginning of the play
    - How Macbeth's behaviour changes through the play
    - The language Shakespeare uses to present Macbeth's character.

3. Write about how women are important in *A View from the Bridge*.
    You may wish to think about:
    - The character of Beatrice
    - The character of Catherine
    - The relationships between men and women.

4. Write about the relationship between Othello and Desdemona in *Othello.*
    You may wish to think about:
    - Their relationship at the beginning of the play
    - Their relationship at the end and how it has changed
    - The language Shakespeare uses to describe their relationship.

N.B. If you aren't studying any of these texts, don't worry — the practice exam paper at the end of the book has more texts to choose from.

What You Have To Do

Poetry questions often follow the <u>same</u> pattern — learn <u>how</u> to answer them and you'll bag big marks.

Break the **Question** into **Parts**

When you're working out what to write about, underline key words in the question so they <u>stand out</u>.

This is the <u>instruction</u>.

This is the <u>topic</u>.

<u>Compare</u> how <u>feelings about relationships</u> are shown in 'Praise Song for My Mother' and <u>one other poem</u> from 'Relationships'.
Remember to compare: • <u>the feelings</u> in the texts
                      • <u>how these feelings are shown</u>

You need to write about <u>two poems</u> to get a good grade.

The bullet points tell you <u>what to write about</u>.

You need to think about these **Things**

1) Your <u>opinion</u> and <u>ideas</u> about the poem.
2) How <u>structure</u>, <u>form</u> and <u>language</u> are used to show <u>ideas</u> and <u>themes</u>.
3) <u>Similarities</u> and <u>differences</u> between poems and their <u>effect</u> on the reader.

Support what you say with <u>examples</u> from the poems.

You'll **Always** have to write about **Language**

The question might ask you <u>directly</u> about language —

> Compare the poets' choice of language in 'Hour' and one other poem.

The question might be <u>worded differently</u>, but it still <u>wants you</u> to talk about language —

These both want you to write about the poets' use of language.

> Write about how the poets show these feelings to the reader.

> Write about the ways in which these ideas are presented.

Read the question really carefully...

Make sure you follow the <u>instructions</u> in the question. If it says "Write about 'Wind' by Ted Hughes and one other poem", then <u>just</u> writing about 'Wind' will mean you <u>miss out</u> on marks.

What You Have To Do

Poetry can be <u>tricky</u>, but there are some things you can do in your <u>essay</u> to earn great marks.

Be Clear and *Back Up* your points

1) Use <u>short quotes</u> from the text to back up your points. Remember to explain what they show.

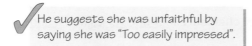 He suggests she was unfaithful by saying she was "Too easily impressed".

instead of

 He thinks she was unfaithful.

2) Make <u>clear</u>, <u>definite</u> statements.

 'Futility' <u>is</u> a poem about conflict

instead of

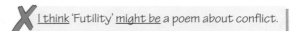 <u>I think</u> 'Futility' <u>might be</u> a poem about conflict.

You'll have to **Compare** *different poems*

<u>Comparing</u> means finding <u>similarities</u> and <u>differences</u> between two or more poems.
You could say something like:

> In 'Sonnet 116', Shakespeare says that love doesn't change when beauty fades. However, in 'To His Coy Mistress', Marvell says that it's best to love before you become old and less attractive.

Show that you **Understand** *what the poet is doing*

1) Show that you can <u>put yourself in the poet's place</u> and <u>understand</u> what they're feeling.

2) Write about how <u>the poet</u> feels and how you think they want to make <u>you</u> feel.

Make sure you back up anything you say about the poet with evidence.

Be **Imaginative**

1) Write down your <u>own</u> ideas about the poem, how it makes you <u>feel</u> and what you think it <u>means</u>.

2) Think about <u>other</u> ways that the poem could be <u>interpreted</u> (what else it could mean).

3) There's only one rule — <u>back up</u> your idea with a <u>quote</u> from the text.

Back up each point you make with a quote...

When you're <u>comparing</u> poems, write about <u>similarities</u> and <u>differences</u> between them
— <u>don't</u> just write about one poem, then about the other. See p.67 for more on comparing.

Style and Structure in Poetry

Different structures and styles are used in different kinds of poem...

Learn the different Types of poem

There are different types or forms of poems. Writing about form is a good way to get marks.

Ballads	Ballads have a regular rhythm and tell a story. They often have four-line verses and a chorus.
Elegies	An elegy is written for someone who has died, and is usually quite slow and thoughtful.
Free Verse	Poems written in free verse have lines of uneven length that do not have to rhyme.
Sonnets	Sonnets are usually 14 lines long, with a regular rhyme scheme.

Write about Form and Structure

1) A poem's form is its physical features — for example the number of lines, rhyme and rhythm. Using these words to describe a poem's form shows that you really know your stuff:

> A stanza is the proper word for a verse.   A tercet is a three-line stanza.
> A rhyming couplet is a pair of lines that rhyme.   A quatrain is a four-line stanza.

2) Structure is how the poet arranges the ideas or events in the poem to put them across effectively.

> For example in 'next to of course god america i' by E E Cummings, the final line shows that the speaker is addressing an audience, and is nervous. This makes the reader suspicious of the speaker.

Work out the Voice of the poem

1) First person narration uses "I" and "me". It helps the reader understand the narrator's viewpoint, so it's often used for poems about personal things.
2) Third person narration uses "he" and "she". Third person narration sounds more detached than first person, which makes the reader trust what the narrator's saying.

Remember — poetry has form and structure...

Some poems have forms that are easy to write about (e.g. sonnets). But you can write about any poem's form, even if it's to make the point that it doesn't have a regular one.

Words to Use When Writing about Poetry

Using <u>technical</u> words to write about poetry impresses the <u>examiner</u> and gets you better marks.

Using the **Right Technical Words** will get you marks

For more useful literature words, see p.66.

Alliteration

When letters are repeated, usually at the beginning of words.

The <u>gr</u>eedy <u>g</u>oat <u>g</u>uzzled the <u>gr</u>ass.

Assonance

When vowel sounds are repeated in the middle of words.

The m<u>ou</u>ldy g<u>oa</u>t <u>o</u>nly h<u>o</u>ped to fl<u>oa</u>t.

Enjambment

When a sentence runs from one line of poetry into the next one (this helps to emphasise certain words).

The goat was alone for three hundred thousand years.

This line starts with 'hundred thousand' so the number really stands out.

Onomatopoeia

When a word sounds like the thing it is describing.

Crash, Splat, Bang

Rhythm

The beats within each line (like music). Can be regular or irregular.

regular

irregular

The goat required a field of grass each day.
The goat was so hungry he stuffed his big fat ugly face.

Pace

How quick/slow/clunky/graceful the words actually sound.

"The goat gambolled gracefully over the green, green grass," has a faster pace than, "The goat, which was young, climbed nimbly and gracefully up the craggy mountain."

Tone

What feeling the words are spoken with (e.g. anger, happiness, fear, etc...).

"Only a goat would understand modern art today," (irony).
"If only I hadn't given in to the goat's commands," (regret).

Learn these words to improve your answers...

These words are <u>tricky</u>, but worth <u>learning</u> to help you write about poetry in the exam. But <u>don't</u> use them if you're not sure what they mean. Do come up with your <u>own</u> examples to help you <u>remember</u> them.

Warm-Up Questions and Worked Exam Answer

There's only one way to find out if you've got all this poetry studying in the bag. That's right — warm-up questions, followed by exam questions. There's a worked answer to help, mind.

Warm-Up Questions

1   What is a stanza?

2   Why should you underline the key words in a poetry question?

3   Define alliteration and give an example.

Worked Exam Question

1   Compare the way power is presented in 'My Last Duchess' and **one** other poem you have studied.
Remember to compare:
  • who has power in each poem
  • the way power is presented.

Essay plan:

Intro — power struggle in relationships

1. Power struggle — anger, jealousy in Medusa

2. Power struggle — anger, jealousy in MLD

3. Use of Power — narrator in MLD uses real violence, gains control after death, has control over painting

4. Use of Power — imaginary violence in Medusa, narrator desperate for husband's love

Conclusion — Angry, caring Medusa / Angry, violent MLD

Try to pick out the main focus of your essay in the introduction.

Essay answer:

Both 'My Last Duchess' and 'Medusa' are about <u>power struggles</u> in relationships. In 'Medusa', the narrator is a woman who wants to control her husband's feelings for her, but <u>feels she is powerless</u> to do this. In 'My Last Duchess' we are presented with a man who wants to control his wife's actions, but is <u>powerless</u> over her while she is alive.

Both poets show that a lack of power makes the narrator angry. In Duffy's poem, the narrator imagines she is a

Worked Exam Answer

Try to think beyond the obvious when explaining your quotes.

"Gorgon" with "filthy snakes" for hair. When she looks at herself in the mirror she "stared at a dragon", which is a powerful but violent image. By using the imagery of a dragon and <u>a Gorgon – an Ancient Greek monster – she suggests that she dreams about being more powerful than she is in reality</u>. It allows her to imagine that she can get revenge on her husband because she is jealous that he is unfaithful.

When his wife was alive, Browning's narrator was also jealous and felt a lack of power in his relationship. He was angry because the Duchess's "looks went everywhere" and she was "too soon made glad" as if she showed too much attention to other men, and this "disgusts" him. The strong, <u>emotive</u> word "disgusts" stands out because the rest of the language in the poem is so formal.

You'll impress the examiner if you use technical terms in the right way.

However, in 'My last Duchess' the Duke goes on to suggest that he is no longer powerless. The line <u>"I gave commands / Then all smiles stopped"</u>, suggests that he has now gained power by ordering for the Duchess to be killed. Controlling the painting of her also makes him feel powerful, "none puts by / The curtain I have drawn for you, but I". It is only possible for the Duke to have power over his wife after she has died — while she was alive, she was the one with the power.

Use plenty of quotes to back up your points.

Don't forget to keep pointing out similarities and differences between the poems.

<u>In contrast with the Duke in 'My Last Duchess', the narrator in 'Medusa' only has imaginary power</u>. At the end of the poem, the narrator's language becomes desperate as she asks "Wasn't I beautiful? / Wasn't I fragrant and young?". This shows that she is dependent on her husband's love for her. Her husband has "a shield" and "a sword" which suggests that he is the one who holds the power in the relationship.

Try to sum up your overall thoughts about the two poems in your conclusion.

<u>Both poems present a struggle for power in a relationship.</u> The main difference is that in 'Medusa' the narrator realises she has no real power and is left pleading with her husband for his attention. In 'My Last Duchess', the narrator is finally able to control the Duchess, though it is suggested that he gains power through shocking violence.

Exam Questions

<u>You are allowed to use the text to write your essay.</u>

1   Describe the writer's thoughts and feelings about pride and power in 'Ozymandias'.

2   Describe the writer's attitude towards war in 'The Charge of the Light Brigade'.

3   Describe the writer's feelings about love in 'To His Coy Mistress'.

4   People often have different opinions about poems. Compare your response to two poems that you've been studying in class. Say whether you like the poems or not, and back up your answer with evidence from the poems.

N.B. If you aren't studying any of these texts, don't worry — the practice exam paper at the end of the book has more texts to choose from.

What You Have To Do

When you write about prose, you still need to write about themes, characters and language.

Write a bit about When it was Written

1) You often have to show you know when the text was written, and what significance this has. There's more on how to do this further down this page.

2) Some books are set during the time they were written. Other books are set in a different time.

3) Authors often express opinions about important issues of the time but do this through imaginative characters or settings.

4) This means the author can write about present-day issues without criticising anyone directly.

> George Orwell wrote Animal Farm in 1945. It tells the story of a bunch of pigs who take over a farm. It's not actually about pigs though — it's about events which took place around that time in Russia.

Show you Understand the Issues being dealt with

1) Texts can address social issues:

> 'Robin Hood' is concerned with poverty.

2) They can have historical themes:

> Different versions of 'Robin Hood' have different interpretations of the role the royal family played at that time.

3) They can have a moral message:

> 'Robin Hood' portrays theft and mugging as acceptable, if it's for a good cause.

Write in Detail

Most questions ask you to comment on how a writer has shown the reader things.

Personality of a character	Experiences of characters	Attitudes of characters

Conflicts between characters	Message and meaning of the text as a whole

Make notes about the issues in a text before the exam...

If you notice something (about language, a character etc.) while you're reading a text, make a note of it. It's good to be original, as long as it's relevant to the question and backed up with a quote.

What You Have To Do

Read the question carefully, so you don't go barking up the wrong tree.

Questions about the Message can look daunting

This is the kind of question you might get:

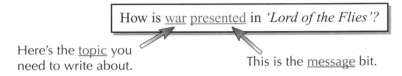

How is <u>war</u> <u>presented</u> in *'Lord of the Flies'?

Here's the <u>topic</u> you need to write about.

This is the <u>message</u> bit.

In questions about the message, <u>always</u> write about <u>what the writer is trying to say</u>.

> Golding suggests in *Lord of the Flies* that war is inevitable. We can tell this because...

Some questions ask about a Specific chunk of Text

Some questions will quote a <u>page or so</u> of one of your <u>set texts</u> and ask you about it.

If you're answering a question on an <u>extract</u>, talk about these <u>3 things</u>:

> 1) How is the extract relevant to the rest of the text?
> 2) Why is it important?
> 3) How are language, structure and form used in the extract?

You might have to write about Style

Some questions will ask you about the <u>writing style</u>.

Your answer will be about the usual style things (e.g. language, imagery, tone — see p.64). Remember — don't talk about these things as if they just happen <u>by accident</u>.

Let the examiner know that you understand it's <u>all done by the writer</u>.

> The <u>writer uses</u> symbolism in this section to show us that... ✓

> The symbolism could help the writer to show the reader that... ✗

Don't just write about your favourite topic — answer the question...

Before you write a prose essay, <u>read</u> the question really carefully. <u>Underline</u> the most important bits, and then <u>plan</u> your answer. Always keep the <u>question</u> in mind to make sure you're answering it.

Writing about Writers

If you're asked how the writer shows the reader something, you'll need to know this stuff.

How does the writer put the text together?

Think about these questions if you get asked how the writer communicates with the reader.

| How are the paragraphs structured? | → | In what order is the information given to you? |

| What language have they used? | → | Why has the writer used one word and not another? |

| Who is the narrator? | → | Why have they chosen to write from a certain viewpoint? |

| How has the writer used imagery? | → | What pictures have they created in your mind? Why have they done this? |

Why does the writer choose one way over another?

Writing is all about finding the best way to tell your story.

There's no right or wrong way to structure a book or use language — only what's appropriate.

> Meera Syal uses Midlands dialect words in *Anita and Me*, which makes the book's main characters seem more real.

> Allan Stratton wrote *Chanda's Secrets* in the first person. This helps us to understand the viewpoint of Chanda, the main character.

What is the writer trying to do?

1) Show the examiner you understand that short stories and novels have been thought up and written by the writer, and that they're trying to make you think in a particular way.

2) You can show that you are aware of this by referring to the writer. For example:

> In 'Paddy Clarke Ha Ha Ha', Roddy Doyle tells the story from Paddy's point of view. This means we see the behaviour and problems of the adult characters through a child's eyes.

Think about how the writer writes, and why...

It's tempting to think that the writer just sits down one day with a cup of tea and a chocolate digestive and starts writing whatever comes into their head, but it doesn't actually work like that.

Questions about Characters

Character questions come up a lot. You need to be able to write about characters confidently.

Prepare *for character questions*

Make revision notes on the points below for the texts you're studying.
Not all of these will apply so pick the ones that fit best.

Why *is a character important?*

> Think about how each character affects the plot and what would happen if
> they weren't there. E.g. in 'Of Mice and Men', would Lennie and George
> have achieved their dream if Curly's wife hadn't been living on the farm?

Does *the character change or learn something?*

1) Characters often change during the text.
2) For example, in 'Lord of the Flies' Jack becomes more savage after he paints a mask on his face.
3) Has the character learnt something that's changed their actions or opinions?

How *does the writer reveal a character's personality?*

1) Does the reader see a character in the same way as other characters in the book?
2) Do the characters relate well to each other or do they have differences in personality? (e.g. Jack and Ralph in 'Lord of the Flies'). What does the writer want these differences to show us?
3) Does a character have a particular point of view?

What *does the writer want us to think about a character?*

1) How do you feel about each character, e.g. do you sympathise with them? Why?
2) How has the writer used language and structure to make you feel that way?

Learning about characters is an important part of your revision...

There's a good chance there'll be a question on characters in the exam so it's best to prepare for one.
Knowing all the characters inside out will also help you to understand what's going on in the text.

Warm-Up Questions and Worked Exam Answer

It might seem like hard work, but doing practice exam questions is the best way to make sure you've learnt this section. Don't panic just yet — here are some lovely warm-up questions and a worked example to make sure you're fully prepared for the exam questions over the page.

Warm-Up Questions

1   If the question asks you about the context of a book, should you talk about the times when it was written? Why/why not?

2   Are the writer and the narrator the same person:
    a)   in a novel written in the <u>third person</u>?
    b)   in a novel written in the <u>first person</u>?

3   Fill in the gaps in this sentence with words from the box:
    Quoting to _____ your points is _____ in any English Literature essay.

stupid	support	not important	very important

4   If they ask you to write about an extract from a book in the exam, should you:
    a) just write about the part of the book that's quoted and ignore the rest of the book
    b) mention a couple of things that happen in the book so it looks like you've read all of it
    c) write about how this extract fits in with the rest of the book and why it's important.

Worked Exam Question

1   How does Harper Lee present Atticus as a good father in *To Kill a Mockingbird*? In your answer you should consider:

    •   How Atticus brings up Jem and Scout
    •   How he sets a good example for his children
    •   How Jem and Scout feel about Atticus.

    Shows that narrator's viewpoint is important to how character is presented

    Essay plan:

    1.   *Introduction — Comment on Scout as narrator — Atticus is presented from his child's point of view so sounds convincing*

    2.   *Examples of how he treats them*

    3.   *Mention what he teaches them (by example) about morals and compare to others who are bad examples*

    4.   *It is a realistic presentation because he makes mistakes (like believing Bob Ewell won't attack him or the children)*

    Important to refer to the writer's aims

    5.   *Conclusion — Harper Lee ends the book with a scene focused on how Atticus makes Scout feel safe — this shows that Atticus' role as a father is very important to the novel as a whole.*

Worked Exam Answer

Essay:

Harper Lee uses Atticus' daughter Scout to narrate the novel. This means Atticus is presented through Scout's opinion of him. As she is his daughter, we trust Scout's description of Atticus as a father. It also means that the reader is shown several personal moments. For example, Scout describes how Atticus "put his arms around me and rocked me gently", which shows he is kind and reassuring.

Start with a brief description of the writer's methods.

It's good to use quotes to support your points.

Atticus is presented as firm with his children. When Jem ruins Mrs Dubose's garden he tells him off with a voice "like the winter wind". He then makes Jem read regularly to Mrs Dubose as an apology. He does this to teach Jem a lesson about treating people fairly, but also because he wants Jem "to see what real courage is".

Atticus is a good father because he teaches the children about morals. He teaches Scout how important it is to understand another person, telling her to "climb into his skin and walk around in it". This shows how Atticus is able to give his children good moral advice in simple, child-friendly language. Other people also teach the children morals, for example, Miss Gates says it is wrong to be prejudiced and Americans "don't believe in persecuting anybody". However, she doesn't lead by example because she says that the black community was "gettin' way above themselves" which shows her prejudice. In comparison, Atticus doesn't just tell his children what to do, he shows them what is right through his actions. It's important to him that his children have "some feeling that I didn't let you down", so he always does what he thinks is right.

When you give your opinion on the character, remember to give reasons.

A good way to talk about the character in the question is to compare them to others in the novel.

Though Atticus is presented as a good father, he is not presented as an unrealistic, perfect one. He does make mistakes, like not believing Bob Ewell's threats, because he prefers to see the best in people. This generous viewpoint stops him from protecting his children, and Bob Ewell eventually attacks them. Showing Atticus making mistakes creates a more believable character.

Ultimately, the reader believes Atticus is a good father because he makes Scout feel safe and loved. The last sentence of the novel is about Atticus as a father: "He would be there all night, and he would be there when Jem waked up in the morning." By ending the book this way, Harper Lee shows the reader that Atticus' reassuring, safe presence is an important, positive influence in his children's lives.

Try to refer back to the question in your conclusion.

Talking about the writer shows you understand their aims.

Exam Questions

<u>You are allowed to use the text to write your essay.</u>

1   *Animal Farm* by George Orwell
    What different impressions do you get of Snowball in the novel?

    Write about:
    •   Positive impressions of Snowball
    •   Negative impressions of Snowball

2   *Lord of the Flies* by William Golding
    Show how order changes to chaos in the novel.

    Write about:
    •   How order is presented at the beginning of the novel
    •   How order changes to chaos later in the novel

3   *Of Mice and Men* by John Steinbeck
    Consider the theme of loneliness in the novel.

    Write about:
    •   How loneliness is presented
    •   How it affects the relationships and friendships in the novel

4   *Touching the Void* by Joe Simpson
    How is the friendship between Joe and Simon presented in the book?

    Write about:
    •   What their friendship is like before the rope is cut
    •   How both men feel after Simon cuts the rope

N.B. If you aren't studying any of these texts, don't worry — the practice exam paper at the end of the book has more texts to choose from.

Revision Summary

Well, that's another big chunk under your belt. If you can remember the big areas you have to include when you do each kind of essay, that's a good start. But you do have to go into a bit of depth and detail to score the good marks. Go through these questions and make sure you know your stuff.

Drama
1) Which three things do you need to show you understand when writing about a play?
2) What is the name for a play that's supposed to make you laugh?
3) What is dialogue?
4) What are stage directions?
5) Are most lines in a Shakespeare play written in:
   a) rap,
   b) blank verse,
   c) prose?

Poetry
1) True or false? 'You'll always have to write about the language in poetry essays.'
2) Is it a good idea to be imaginative in a poetry essay? Why / why not?
3) How many lines does a sonnet usually have?
4) Stanza is the proper name for:
   a) a verse,
   b) a poem,
   c) a line,
   d) a word?
5) What is:
   a) pace,
   b) alliteration,
   c) enjambment?

Prose
1) Which of these things do you not need to look out for in a text:
   a) Social issues
   b) Snotty tissues
   c) Historical themes
   d) Moral issues?
2) When you're answering a question about the message of a text, do you need to write about:
   a) what the writer is trying to say,
   b) whether you enjoyed the novel or not?
3) Which of these sentences about a writer's style is better? Why?
   a) 'The imagery creates a vivid impression of the setting.'
   b) 'The writer uses imagery to create a vivid impression of the setting.'
4) Give two things you could mention if you're writing about how the text is put together.
5) How can you show that you're aware of what the writer's trying to do?
6) Name four key points that you could include in your revision notes about characters in a novel.

Make Your Writing Clear to Read

A big chunk of the marks for a writing exam question are for how you write, not what you write about.

Writing *Well* gets you a better grade

This is what you'll be marked on:

1) Standard English (see p.92)
    Unless you're writing in the voice of a character, examiners will expect you to
    use Standard English. Don't slip into slang or local dialect, or you'll lose marks.

2) Punctuation (see p.93-95)
    Punctuation is brilliant for making your writing smooth, clear and punchy —
    but only if you get it right. Make sure you know when to use commas, apostrophes etc.

3) Spelling and types of words (see p.98-100)
    Your spelling needs to be pretty accurate if you want a good grade,
    and it also helps if you know how to use different types of words correctly.

4) Sentence types (see p.101)
    Use a mixture of sentence structures — from short and simple to long and complex.

5) Using varied language (see p.102-3)
    Use similes and metaphors when you're describing something,
    and make sure you use some interesting words too.

6) Paragraphs (see p.5-6)
    Writing in paragraphs is very important for organising your writing into manageable sections.

Writing bad English don't get you nowhere...

If you learn the rules in this section and use them when you're writing, you won't go too far wrong.
Make sure you check your work before you hand it in, so you can correct any obvious mistakes.

Standard English

The examiners want you to use Standard English, so you'll lose marks if you don't know how...

Use Standard English

1) People in different areas use different local words (dialect) that can be hard for others to understand.
2) Standard English avoids any dialect words and is understood by people all over the country.

Using Standard English means following some Simple Rules

1) Don't write the informal words you'd say when talking to your friends, e.g. 'OK', 'yeah'.
2) Don't use slang, local dialect words or text speak.
3) Use correct spelling and grammar.

Avoid these Common Mistakes

RULE: Don't put the word 'them' in front of names of objects — always use 'those'.

Let me see them books. ✗   Let me see those books. ✓

RULE: 'Who' is used to talk about people. 'That' or 'which' is used for everything else.

King Lear had two daughters who lied to him.

Percy met a lion that did not kill him.
OR
Percy met a lion which did not kill him.

Either 'that' or 'which' is fine.

RULE: Don't write 'like' when you mean 'as'.

Othello did like Iago told him. ✗

This sounds much better. → Othello did as Iago told him. ✓

If you're writing to the Prime Minister — be formal...

Another thing the examiners, like, really hate is if you, like, keep using the word 'like' when you, like, don't need it. Only use informal language like this if it's suitable for a character's speech.

Punctuation

Punctuation isn't just there to make your essays look <u>pretty</u> — it makes your writing a lot <u>clearer</u>.

Start and *Finish* your sentences correctly

Always <u>start</u> sentences with a <u>capital letter</u>. Sentences always <u>end</u> with either:

1) a full stop — use these for most sentences.   →   •

2) a question mark — use these if the sentence is asking a question.   →   **?**

3) an exclamation mark — use these if you want your sentence to have a strong impact.   →   **!**

Use *Commas* to put *Pauses* in sentences

1) Commas <u>separate</u> the parts of long sentences to make the meaning clear.

 In the valley below, the villages all seemed very small.

   Without the comma, the sentence would
   begin 'in the valley below the villages'.

2) Commas are also used to break up the items in a <u>list</u>:

 I bought onions, mushrooms, peppers and pasta.

3) <u>Pairs of commas</u> can be used to add <u>extra information</u> to the <u>middle</u> of sentences:

 The twins, <u>who had their blue wigs on</u>, were eating seaweed.

    comma   comma

   The sentence would still work
   without the bit in the middle.

You need to learn this stuff on punctuation — full stop...

It's really <u>difficult</u> to read a text with no punctuation at all, so you've got to use it in the exam.
When you finish your writing, <u>check</u> it to make sure there aren't any <u>silly</u> mistakes in it.

Apostrophes

Apostrophes can seem <u>tricky</u>, but they're not actually too difficult if you stick to a few <u>simple rules</u>...

Add *'s* to show *Who Owns* something

The dog belongs to Montel so you add an <u>apostrophe</u> + '<u>s</u>' to the name of the owner.

> Montel's dog is less scary now.

There's a catch, though:

> <u>Its</u> = something <u>belongs</u> to <u>it</u>.
> <u>Its</u> doesn't follow the apostrophe rule.

> The dog has had its dinner.

It gets a bit *Tricky* with *Groups of People* or *Things*

> They found the killer <u>eels</u>' lair during the <u>men's</u> underwater race.

1) If it already ends in <u>s</u>, stick an apostrophe on the <u>end</u> but <u>not</u> an extra <u>s</u>.

2) Plural words that don't end in s, e.g. <u>men</u> and <u>mice</u>, follow the normal rule of apostrophe + '<u>s</u>'.

Apostrophes can show where there's a *Missing Letter*

1) You can <u>shorten</u> some pairs of words by sticking them together and cutting out letters.
2) You put an <u>apostrophe</u> to show where you've removed the letters from.

E.g. I am ⟹ I'm   The letter 'a' has been removed, so an apostrophe goes <u>in its place</u>.

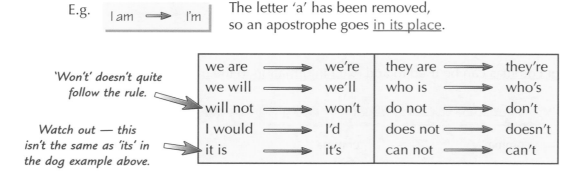

'Won't' doesn't quite follow the rule.

Watch out — this isn't the same as 'its' in the dog example above.

we are ⟶ we're	they are ⟶ they're
we will ⟶ we'll	who is ⟶ who's
will not ⟶ won't	do not ⟶ don't
I would ⟶ I'd	does not ⟶ doesn't
it is ⟶ it's	can not ⟶ can't

Impress the examiner — use apostrophes properly...

And now, a word of <u>warning</u> — never, <u>ever</u> use an apostrophe to show that something's <u>plural</u> (for example: two banana's, five pear's). I know your greengrocer does it, but that doesn't make it right.

Speech Marks

You guessed it — speech marks are yet another thing the examiner will be <u>looking out for</u>.

Speech Marks show someone's *Actually Speaking*

Start of speech   End of speech

"You're going to lose that pretty hat," said Bob.

These are the words Bob said — they go in the <u>quotation marks</u>, or <u>speech marks</u>.

Always *Start Speech* with a *Capital Letter*

"<u>L</u>et's have a game of pogo-stick golf," said Claude.

Here's the <u>capital letter</u>.

The speech bit <u>always</u> begins with a capital letter — even if it isn't at the start of the sentence.

Doug asked, "<u>W</u>here's the nineteenth hole?"

"My pogo stick," Claude boasted, "<u>i</u>s brand new."

If a speech is split into two sections, you <u>don't</u> need a capital letter at the start of the second section.

End speech with a *Question Mark*, *Full Stop* or *Comma*

"Who will fight me in a duel<u>?</u>" asked Louise.

Remember — <u>questions</u> need a question mark.

Marco shouted, "I'm not afraid to fight<u>!</u>"

Marco's shouting, so this should end with an <u>exclamation mark</u>.

"You're no match for me<u>,</u>" replied Louise bravely<u>.</u>

The speech has finished but the sentence hasn't — you need a <u>comma</u> here.

The sentence finishes here, so you need a <u>full stop</u>.

These rules may seem tricky, but they're really useful...

The punctuation rules are well worth <u>learning</u> because they're exactly the same when you're <u>quoting</u> from a <u>text</u> in a literature essay. Try practising them by writing about a <u>conversation</u> with a friend.

Negatives

It's a page about <u>negatives</u> — deep breath, chin up and don't let it get you down.

'No' Isn't the only Negative word

The easiest way to make a phrase negative is to add '<u>no</u>' or '<u>not</u>' (or by adding <u>-n't</u> to a word, see p.94).

Positive sentence: My aubergines are rotten.

Negative sentence: My aubergines are <u>not</u> rotten.

Don't use Double Negatives

<u>Two negative words</u> in the same phrase will make it <u>positive</u>, e.g.:

I <u>don't</u> want <u>no</u> aubergine.   REALLY MEANS   I <u>do</u> want some aubergine.

Only use <u>one negative</u> at a time. I <u>don't</u> want any aubergine.

The word None has different meanings

1) '<u>None</u>' can cause problems, because it has different meanings.

It can mean 'not one':   <u>None</u> of the students passed the test.

It can also mean 'not any':   I want an aubergine, but there are <u>none</u> left.

2) The main thing you need to remember is that 'none' should <u>not</u> be used with other negative words:

He has <u>not</u> got <u>none</u>.   He has <u>none</u>.

Stop being so negative — it's not that bad...

Negative sentences can be very <u>useful</u> in your writing and can make it sound more <u>interesting</u>.
Remember the points on this page to help you collect some <u>positive</u> marks in your exams.

Warm-Up Questions

You could read through this page in a few minutes but there's no point unless you check over any bits you don't know and make sure you understand everything. It's not quick, but it's the only way.

Warm-Up Questions

1) Which of these should you check for when you finish a piece of writing?
   a) correct punctuation
   b) cauliflowers
   c) paragraphs properly divided up
   d) spelling all right
   e) each sentence grammatical
   f) bookworms

2) What is 'Standard English'?

3) Do you need to use Standard English in your GCSE exam?

4) Can you think of any parts of your English GCSE when it would be all right <u>not</u> to use Standard English?

5) Choose the grammatically correct sentence in each of the following pairs:
   a) *Give me them pens.*
      or *Give me those pens.*
   b) *Macbeth is a general who kills a king.*
      or *Macbeth is a general which kills a king.*
   c) *The boy did as the teacher said.*
      or *The boy did like the teacher said.*

6) What do you <u>always</u> have to have at the beginning of a sentence?

7) What are the three things you can use to finish your sentence?

8) Write down three ways you can use a comma.

9) Write out these sentences with the correct punctuation:
   a) the man who still hadnt recovered from his cold was feeling ill
   b) i need to buy chicken cherries chocolate cheese and chips
   c) why wont Roberts dog play with the childrens dog
   d) Sarah asked has anyone seen Liz today
   e) does anyone want another cup of tea Andy asked because Im having one

10) What will the examiners think you mean if you write 'I don't want to do no English exam'?

11) Write out these sentences and add in the apostrophes you need.
    a) Charlies dogs were eating bananas.
    b) I dont like Franks new trousers.
    c) Mum says its going to rain today.

Spelling

Some spelling mistakes are really <u>common</u> — luckily this page tells you how to <u>avoid</u> making them.

Don't confuse **Different** words that **Sound** the **Same**

Two words that sound similar can mean different things. Here are some common examples to look out for:

1) affect / effect

1) <u>Affect</u> means 'to influence something'. ⟹ Burning fossil fuels <u>affects</u> the Earth's climate.
2) An <u>effect</u> is the result of an action. ⟹ The <u>effect</u> of burning fossil fuels is global warming.

2) there / their / they're

1) <u>There</u> is used to talk about <u>place</u>. ⟹ The ball is over <u>there</u>.
2) <u>Their</u> shows that someone <u>owns</u> something. ⟹ <u>Their</u> dog bit me!
3) <u>They're</u> is the short form of '<u>they are</u>'. ⟹ <u>They're</u> my favourite shoes.

3) where / were / wear

1) <u>Where</u> is used to talk about <u>place</u>. ⟹ <u>Where</u> is the Frenchman?
2) <u>Were</u> is the past tense of the verb '<u>to be</u>'. ⟹ They <u>were</u> hidden behind a statue.
3) <u>Wear</u> is what you do with clothes, shoes etc. ⟹ He wants to <u>wear</u> his new bow tie.

4) your / you're

1) <u>Your</u> means something that belongs to <u>you</u>. ⟹ Hand me <u>your</u> homework.
2) <u>You're</u> is the short form of '<u>you are</u>'. ⟹ <u>You're</u> not allowed to eat that in here.

Watch out for these **Common Spelling Mistakes**

1) Words with a <u>silent 'h'</u> — you don't say it, but you must write it: e.g. <u>c</u>hemistry.
2) Words written with '<u>ph</u>' and pronounced with an 'f' sound: e.g. gra<u>ph</u> or <u>ph</u>iloso<u>ph</u>y.
3) Words with an '<u>i</u>' before an '<u>e</u>' except <u>after 'c'</u>: e.g. rel<u>ie</u>f or rec<u>ei</u>ve
4) Words where the <u>endings change</u> when they're made <u>plural</u>: e.g. bab<u>ies</u> not bab<u>ys</u>.

Get your spelling write...

You need to know how to spell the <u>names</u> of writers and the <u>title</u> of any books, poems and plays you're studying. Take a look at p.66 and p.79 for more words that you should learn how to spell.

Nouns, Verbs, Adverbs and Adjectives

You need to know the proper <u>names</u> for the different <u>types</u> of words, so get your learning hat on.

A **Noun** is a **Person**, **Place** or **Thing**

There are four kinds of noun:

1) '<u>Proper</u>' names (towns, people, months etc.), e.g. Gloria, Sunday, Texas.
2) <u>Groups</u> of people or things, e.g. class, pack, squad.
3) <u>Names</u> of other <u>everyday things</u>, e.g. hedge, hair, woman.
4) Words for <u>ideas</u>, e.g. truth, beauty, fear.

Proper names always have <u>capital letters</u>.

Verbs are 'Doing' or 'Being' words

'Doing' words

riding   thinks
ate   bounces

'Doing' words tell you <u>what's happening</u> in a sentence.

'Being' words

Today **was** good.
I **am** happy.

'Being' words tell you how something <u>is</u> or <u>was</u> or <u>will be</u>.

Adjectives describe **Things** and **People**

Global warming is <u>bad</u>. ✗

Too boring — <u>zero marks alert</u>!

Global warming is a <u>serious</u> and <u>worrying</u> issue. ✓

Much better — the <u>adjectives</u> will impress the examiner.

Adverbs describe **How** an **Action** is done

The tree <u>fell</u>, <u>missing</u> my leg. ✗

Boring — the <u>verbs</u> have been left plain.

The tree fell <u>suddenly</u>, <u>narrowly</u> missing my leg. ✓

The <u>adverbs</u> make the sentence more <u>exciting</u>.

Variety is the spice of English essays...

Use different <u>verbs</u>, <u>adjectives</u> and <u>adverbs</u> in your writing and don't repeat the same word too much. This will help make your writing more <u>interesting</u>, and bag you loads of marks from the examiner.

Using Verbs in Sentences

The message of this page is that your sentences need to <u>make sense</u>. Simple, but very important.

Every sentence needs a **Verb**

1) Verbs are '<u>doing</u>' words or '<u>being</u>' words (see p.99) — and <u>every</u> sentence needs to have one.
2) The form of the verb <u>changes</u> depending on <u>when</u> the action takes place.

In the past:

I <u>was</u> the world's first snail-tamer.

In the future:

I <u>will be</u> the world's first snail-tamer.

These are both '<u>being</u>' words — but they're in different tenses.

Make sure you use the **Right Form** *of the verb*

1) Every <u>verb</u> describes what someone (or something) is <u>doing</u> (or <u>being</u>).
2) If there's only <u>one person</u> doing something, use the <u>singular</u> form of the verb.
3) If there's <u>more than one person</u> doing something, use the <u>plural</u> form of the verb.
4) When you're writing a verb in a sentence, say it <u>out loud</u>. Decide whether it <u>sounds right</u> or not.

They <u>was</u> eating mouse sandwiches. ✗

This sounds wrong. '<u>They</u>' means more than one person, so the subject is <u>plural</u>.

They <u>were</u> eating mouse sandwiches. ✓

Much better — that sounds right and it makes sense too.

Don't *change* ***When Things Happen*** *in your writing by* ***Mistake***

This is in the <u>past</u>.   Another <u>past</u> verb.

As they <u>tried</u> to get the sail up, they <u>could</u> hear distant splashes — then they <u>see</u> a canoe.

This one's <u>wrong</u> — it's in the <u>present</u> when it should be <u>past</u> (i.e. 'they <u>saw</u> a canoe').

Sentences don't have to be complicated — but they have to be right...

These three rules are very important. It's good to write <u>longer</u>, more <u>complicated</u> sentences, but they still have to be <u>correct</u>. When you finish writing an answer, <u>check</u> your sentences make sense.

Sentences

If you really want to wow the examiner, you'll need to use different <u>types</u> of <u>sentences</u>.

Vary the Style of your sentences

Using <u>different sentence types</u> will make your writing more <u>interesting</u>. For example:

<u>Simple</u> sentences are good for <u>emphasising</u> important points. ⟹ *My cat likes Mexican food.*

Try adding another part in the <u>middle</u> of the sentence. ⟹ *My cat, <u>who has a wonky tail</u>, likes Mexican food.*

Or add <u>another part</u> to the sentence and join it to the first part using a word like <u>and</u> or <u>but</u>. ⟹ *My cat likes Mexican food, <u>but he won't eat curry</u>.*

Start your sentences in *Different Ways*

Your writing will be pretty <u>boring</u> if all your sentences start with the same words. For example:

<u>There was</u> a chill in the air as Jo walked towards the house. <u>There was</u> nobody around. <u>There was</u> a big oak door and Jo knocked on it. <u>There was</u> a scream from inside the house.

It's much <u>more interesting</u> if you <u>vary</u> the way you start sentences:

There was a chill in the air as Jo walked towards the house. Nobody was around. Jo knocked on the big oak door. A scream came from inside the house. ✓

Write your sentences in a *Logical Order*

If you write your sentences in the wrong order, your work will be hard to understand. For example:

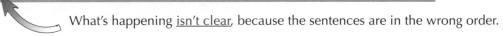

When Harry left the shop, his bike had vanished. Harry went into a shop to get some chocolate.

What's happening <u>isn't clear</u>, because the sentences are in the wrong order.

Try to mix up the style of your sentences...

It can also be really effective to include the occasional <u>rhetorical question</u> (p.37) in your writing — it can help the reader feel more <u>involved</u> and keep them interested in what they're reading.

Writing Varied Sentences

When you're <u>describing</u> something you need to paint a <u>picture</u> in your reader's head — here's how.

Describe things by **Comparing** *them to* **Other Things**

Comparing your subject to something else helps readers to imagine it.
There are <u>three</u> ways of comparing:

1) Using less than, more than, the least, the most...

> She was beautiful. $\Longrightarrow$ She was the <u>most beautiful</u> woman this side of Stockport.

2) You can also say something is <u>more than</u> or <u>the most</u> by adding '<u>er</u>' or '<u>est</u>' to the end, e.g. small<u>er</u>, kind<u>est</u>. But do this instead of using 'more than' or 'most'.

> Jenny is <u>more prettier than</u> her sister.    Jenny is <u>prettier than</u> her sister. ✓

3) Using <u>similes</u> (to say that one thing is <u>like</u> another). You can use the words 'like' or 'as':

> My fingers were <u>like</u> blocks of ice.   Beth felt <u>as</u> happy <u>as</u> a hippo in a mud pool.

Metaphors can create **Strong Images**

1) A <u>metaphor</u> describes one thing as if it <u>is</u> something else.
2) Metaphors can have a <u>very powerful effect</u>.

For more on similes, metaphors and other useful literature words, see p.66.

> Leela cried so hard that a river flowed down her cheeks.

There wasn't really a river flowing down Leela's cheeks, but the language creates a <u>strong visual image</u>.

This page is as useful as a very useful thing...

Using <u>similes</u> and <u>metaphors</u> will make your work really stand out for the examiner. Use your imagination to think of some great <u>images</u> — this'll grab his attention and get you lots of <u>marks</u>.

Writing Varied Sentences

Using lots of <u>different</u> words makes your writing more <u>interesting</u>, which is what the examiner wants...

Use **Different Words** for the **Same Thing**

Don't use the same word all the time — especially vague ones like "<u>nice</u>" or "<u>weird</u>".

| I went to a <u>nice</u> Indian restaurant last night. The waiters were <u>nice</u> to us. I had a <u>nice</u> curry. | | This isn't going to score you many points because it's so <u>boring</u>. |

| This is loads better. Using lots of different adjectives paints a more <u>interesting picture</u>. | | I went to a <u>fantastic</u> Indian restaurant last night. The waiters were <u>friendly</u> to us. I had a <u>delicious</u> curry. |

It's the same with <u>verbs</u> (doing or being words)...

| I <u>ran</u> to the post box with a letter, then I <u>ran</u> to the shop for some chocolate. After that I <u>ran</u> home so I wasn't late for tea. | → | I <u>ran</u> to the post box with a letter, then I <u>hurried</u> to the shop for some chocolate. Finally I <u>raced</u> home so I wasn't late for tea. |

Fancy Words impress the examiner

Using <u>different</u> words is good, but if you're after top marks, try using different <u>and</u> clever words.

| United played <u>badly</u> on Saturday. | | United played <u>dreadfully</u> on Saturday. |

| The referee made some <u>very stupid</u> decisions. | | The referee made some <u>incredibly moronic</u> decisions. |

Remember: it's better to get common words right than get long words wrong. If you're using a different word, make sure you know what it means and how to spell it.

Using the same words all the time is boring...

You shouldn't use long, fancy words <u>all</u> the time — that'd sound daft. But you'll get extra <u>marks</u> if you throw them in every <u>now and then</u>. So, invest in a dictionary and learn some interesting new words.

Warm-Up Questions

Grammar's pretty tricky, so this section has two pages of lovely warm-up questions to make sure you've taken everything in. Have a really good go at them, then check your answers on p.157 and 158.

Warm-Up Questions

1) Choose the correct spelling:
   a) How you spell will <u>affect</u> / <u>effect</u> your grade.
   b) The <u>affects</u> / <u>effects</u> of spelling writers' names wrong can be terrible.

2) Write out these sentences, correcting any errors.
   a) I wish I knew wear I was going, but at least I know were I've been.
   b) If I where to have one wish, it would be that you wear here.

3) Choose the correct sentence from each of the following pairs:
   a) I left my bicycle over their. / I left my bicycle over there.
   b) The twins invited they're friends to tea. / The twins invited their friends to tea.
   c) They're the wrong chickens! / There the wrong chickens!

4) Which of these words is spelled correctly?
   a) height / hieght
   b) athelete / athlete
   c) seene / scene
   d) excercise / exercise?

5) Complete the following sentences by putting the verb into the correct tense:
   a) When I got home, I (turn) _____ the television on.
   b) Today, I (be) _____ happy.

6) Rewrite 5a) and 5b) so they're talking about the future.

7) Put these sentences into the correct order, from the first thing that happened to the last. I left completely satisfied. The crème brulée was the perfect end to a delicious meal, with a silky texture and a diamond-hard crust. We began with a dish of lobster and crayfish which played against the flavours of the champagne like a kitten patting at a butterfly. The beef was perfectly roasted and so tender that I hardly needed to chew.

8) Which of the following sentences sounds more formal?
   a) I go rollerblading now and then. / I go rollerblading occasionally.
   b) Evacuate the building immediately! / Leave the building now!
   c) Fruit and vegetables are extremely nutritious. / Fruit and vegetables are very healthy.

9) Which is correct?
   a) Katy's essay is much more better than Claire's. / Katy's essay is much better than Claire's.
   b) Today was the most hottest day of the year. / Today was the hottest day of the year.
   c) Frank is the tallest twin. / Frank is the taller twin.

10) Pick out the noun, the verb, the adjective and the adverb in each of the following sentences (sometimes there is more than one noun, verb, adjective or adverb):
   a) The enormous horses easily pulled the heavy carriages.
   b) Sonia desperately wanted to know the whole truth.
   c) The naughty little boys waited nervously outside the headteacher's office.

Warm-Up Questions

11) Rewrite this sentence in Standard English — "Nellie loves them cream buns."

12) Insert commas in this sentence so that it makes sense:
   "However the book was written well so I enjoyed it."

13) Correct the mistakes in these sentences:
   a) My sisters hamster has looked very happy since I brushed it's coat.
   b) Its nice to see a smile on its little face.

14) Cut out letters and replace them with apostrophes. The first one is done for you.
   a) I will not = I won't
   b) can not
   c) I would
   d) it is
   e) they are

15) Put the speech marks in the right place in the following sentences:
   a) I really need a holiday, said Martin.
   b) Me too, agreed Chi, I haven't been away for ages.
   c) No, said Pete. Not since that time you were nearly banned from France.

16) Which of these is a negative sentence?
   a) I don't know the answer.
   b) I know the answer.

17) Find the adverbs in these sentences:
   a) I glanced quickly behind me.
   b) I walked nervously down the alley.
   c) The door banged loudly and there was a blinding flash of light.

18) What's wrong with this sentence — "The children only eats sausages"?

19) What three letters could you add to the word "cold" to make it mean "most cold"?

20) What's the difference between a simile and a metaphor? Write an example of each.

21) Are these sentences similes or metaphors?
   a) He was as charming as a sewer rat.
   b) The clouds were a soft, white pillow.
   c) He was a mighty oak and I was just a puny pansy.
   d) The water foamed and boiled like an erupting volcano.

22) Write down three words that mean "bad".

How to Study Spoken Language

This section is about real-life, genuine, home-grown, actual speech — the way people really talk.

Listen Carefully to what People Say

1) The language you use changes depending on what situation you're in and who you're talking to. For example, you call your headmaster 'sir' rather than 'mate'.

2) Pragmatics are hidden or suggested meanings. E.g. you might say to a friend, 'This maths homework's impossible', when what you mean is 'Can you help me with it?'.

3) When you say things like 'yeah' or 'mm' to show someone you're listening, it's called feedback.

Spoken Language is different from Written Language

When people speak naturally, their speech has non-fluency features. Here are some examples:

1) Fillers (e.g. 'er', 'um') — these fill gaps while the speaker thinks of what they want to say.
2) False starts — where the speaker starts saying one thing, then changes their mind.
3) Repetition — people repeat words a lot in unplanned speech, e.g. 'I'm never never going'.
4) Interruption/overlap — people sometimes talk over each other.

Here are some other things you'll hear in real-life speech:

1) Missing words — e.g. 'want to come out' instead of 'do you want to come out'.
2) Slurring words together — e.g. 'gonna' instead of 'going to'.
3) Small talk — phrases that don't have much meaning, e.g. 'Hi, how are you?', or 'Bye'.
4) 'Vague' language — e.g. saying 'sort of', 'like' or 'lots'.
5) Turn-taking — speakers taking it in turns to lead the conversation.

Listen out for How People Speak

1) Stress is when you emphasise certain words to change the meaning of the sentence.
2) Tone of voice can also change the meaning of what you say, e.g. make it playful or sarcastic.
3) Volume can affect meaning — e.g. loudness might show anger, excitement or confidence.

Spoken Language — a bit like written language, only louder...

Blimey. That's an awful lot to think about, but don't worry — it'll make a lot more sense when you start looking at some data and have some sort of context to relate it all to. Trust me, it will.

Social Attitudes to Spoken Language

Some people have <u>strong feelings</u> about the way people speak...

Accents and Dialects can be Regional or Social

An <u>accent</u> is <u>how</u> you say words.

A <u>dialect</u> is the actual <u>words you use</u>.

1) People with different <u>accents pronounce</u> the same words <u>different ways</u>.
2) <u>Regional accents</u> are <u>different</u> depending on which part of the country the speaker's from.
   E.g. people from London sound different from people from Liverpool.
3) A <u>social accent</u> is the result of <u>class</u> or <u>background</u>.

Different Groups Speak Differently from each other

<u>Different groups</u> of people use <u>different language</u> when they're talking.
Middle-aged lawyers will speak <u>differently</u> from teenagers.

1) <u>Sharing</u> group language gives a group an <u>identity</u> — people use it to <u>fit in</u>.
2) Some people think <u>women</u> use more <u>Standard English</u>, and swear and interrupt less than men.
3) <u>Men</u> often use more <u>non-standard grammar</u> and have stronger <u>regional accents</u>.

Idiolect is the Unique way a Person speaks

1) Your individual way of speaking is called your <u>idiolect</u>. Everyone's idiolect is different.
2) It's influenced by the accent and dialect in <u>places you've lived</u> and the <u>people</u> you've spent time with.

Some people think that Non-Standard English is 'Wrong'

1) People have <u>strong opinions</u> about different <u>varieties</u> of English.
2) Some people think that <u>Standard English</u> is 'correct' and other forms are <u>wrong</u>.

But — the type of English that's <u>appropriate</u> depends on what you're doing.
For example, you'd use more <u>slang</u> in an <u>informal chat</u> than in a job interview.

Your parents and teachers don't speak a foreign language...

...but they do use <u>different</u> language to you and your friends. It's important that you know the difference between <u>dialect</u> and <u>accent</u> and understand that not everyone speaks in the same way.

Spoken Genres

Public talk (speeches) and talk in the media is <u>written down</u> to be <u>spoken</u> out loud.

Public Talk is Written to be Spoken

'Public talk' means things like <u>political speeches</u>, or a <u>presentation</u> in a school assembly.
It's written for a specific <u>purpose</u>, and uses some of these techniques:

> 1) Public speakers use <u>Standard English</u> to make their speech sound <u>serious</u> and <u>impressive</u>.
>
> 2) They might use pauses, stress and tone of voice to give the speech <u>meaning</u>.
>
> 3) Individual public speakers and interviewers have their own <u>unique</u> ways of talking, so you could also look at <u>specific speech patterns</u> — e.g. the way someone phrases questions.

You could look at Spoken Language in the Media

1) Things like <u>news reports</u> are planned beforehand to make sure they <u>make sense</u>.
   The presenters on these programmes use <u>Standard English</u>.

2) Language in the media can also be <u>spontaneous</u> (unplanned) — e.g. talk on <u>reality shows</u>.

3) Radio plays and TV soaps and dramas try to sound like <u>real-life talk</u>.
   The actors often have regional accents and might interrupt each other to make it seem <u>realistic</u>.

> Scripted speech is never exactly like real-life talk. If it was then it wouldn't flow, and the audience might miss bits because people were talking at the same time.

Radio Language is Different from TV Language

1) <u>TV language</u> has <u>pictures</u>, <u>gestures</u> and <u>facial expressions</u> to help get the meaning across.

2) On the <u>radio</u>, everything has to be <u>explained</u> using words.

3) Radio presenters have to <u>fill all the silences</u>, so they don't <u>pause</u> very much.

Silence is golden — except if you're talking on the radio...

<u>Spoken</u> language is a funny thing — it's surprisingly <u>hard to mimic</u> the everyday, real-life speech that we hear all the time. Instead, all the talk you hear on the TV and radio sounds a bit more <u>scripted</u>.

Multi-Modal Talk

Multi-modal language is a mixture of written and spoken language.

Modes are different Types of language

1) Written modes include written texts like novels, letters, recipes etc.
2) Spoken modes are things like informal conversations, radio broadcasts and speeches.
3) Multi-modal talk means written conversations that contain elements of spoken language — e.g. using smileys to show what your facial expression would be if you were speaking.

Technology has had a big impact on the amount of multi-modal talk that people use.
In electronic texts like emails, people's writing tends to be less formal and a lot more like speech.

Text Messages and Online Conversations are Multi-Modal

You can have conversations with people via text message or online instant messaging.
These conversations are multi-modal because they can contain lots of 'text speak'.

1) Text speak contains features of spoken language — things like saying 'hi' or 'bye'.
2) Words in text speak often have letters missed out or are replaced with numbers or symbols because it's quicker and cheaper than typing words out in full, e.g.:

> gona be in ldn this wknd if ur around?wud b gr8 2 catch up

3) Online conversation can work like spoken conversation — you take turns and make it clear when it's the other person's go, e.g. by asking them a question.

Some people think Text Speak is 'Bad' English

1) Some people say text speak is hard to understand, and stops people being able to spell properly.
2) Others think it's useful for texts or online chat, but not for other situations.
3) You could argue that language always changes, so text speak is just a natural progression.

Remember mode means type, multi-modal means a mix of types...

It seems like a lot to take in, but a lot of this stuff you'll know all about from experience anyway — it's just a case of learning some fancy terms for things you do every day without knowing it.

Data

You'll probably be <u>given data</u> for your Spoken Language study. Here's a heads up on what to expect.

Your **Data** is the spoken language you'll be **Analysing**

There are all sorts of <u>different types</u> of data that you could get for your controlled assessment:

1) <u>Transcripts</u> of <u>real-life talk</u> (more on transcripts below).
2) <u>Transcripts</u> of <u>audio clips</u> (e.g. a radio show or a TV interview).
3) <u>Text messages</u> or <u>online chat</u> conversations.
4) <u>Scripted</u> language (e.g. a radio advert or public speech).
5) <u>Newspaper articles</u>, or other material that shows <u>people's attitudes</u> to spoken language.

Transcripts look like this

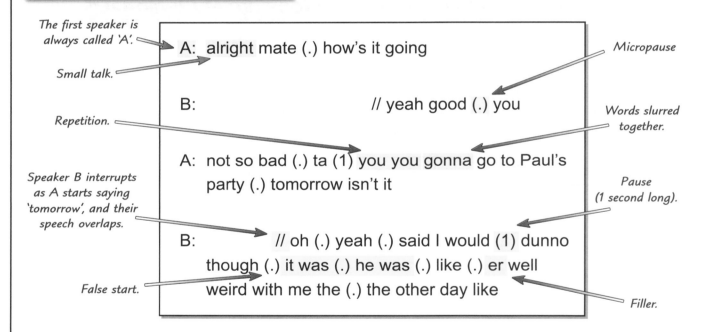

The first speaker is always called 'A'.

Small talk.

A: alright mate (.) how's it going

Micropause

B: // yeah good (.) you

Words slurred together.

Repetition.

A: not so bad (.) ta (1) you you gonna go to Paul's party (.) tomorrow isn't it

Speaker B interrupts as A starts saying 'tomorrow', and their speech overlaps.

Pause (1 second long).

B: // oh (.) yeah (.) said I would (1) dunno though (.) it was (.) he was (.) like (.) er well

False start.

weird with me the (.) the other day like

Filler.

Key

(.) = <u>micropause</u> (less than 1 second)

(2) = a <u>pause</u> showing the number of <u>seconds</u> it lasts (so this one's <u>2 seconds</u> long).

<u>Interruptions</u> or <u>overlap</u> are shown using the symbol // at the point where someone's interrupted.

Learn all the labels on the transcript...

If you're given a <u>transcript</u>, it might not look exactly the same as the one above, but it will be <u>similar</u>. Don't forget that numbers or full stops in brackets are there <u>instead</u> of punctuation.

Writing Up Your Spoken Language Study

Now you know what kind of data you're likely to get, here's how to <u>write</u> about it <u>really well</u>.

Think about **How** you'll **Structure** your **Work**

A <u>three-part</u> structure is best:

 Introduction   Data analysis   ③ Conclusion

When you give in your <u>final essay</u>, make sure you also hand in your <u>data</u> and <u>notes</u>.

Make Sure you have a **Good Introduction**

In your introduction you need to say something about:

1) what <u>kind of spoken language</u> you're looking at.
2) what <u>features</u> of it you're going to discuss.
3) where the <u>data</u> is <u>from</u> — e.g. 'this is a TV interview'.

The **Data Analysis** should be the **Main Bit** of your **Answer**

Use <u>paragraphs</u> to <u>structure</u> your answer. For example, you might have paragraphs about:

- Vocabulary (e.g. slang, jargon, dialect words)
- Accent/dialect
- Grammar (e.g. standard or non-standard)
- Non-fluency features (e.g. pauses, false starts, interruption)
- Elements of spoken language that aren't words (e.g. loudness, stress, tone of voice)

Finish with a **Conclusion**

In your <u>paragraph</u>, you should sum up what you've found out.
Remember to refer back to the <u>question</u> — say what your data shows and how it <u>answers</u> the question.

Make sure your essay has a clear structure...

You get the idea. If you can get a good <u>structure</u> from the start, your answer should fall <u>effortlessly</u> into place. The controlled assessment can be a gold mine of marks if you <u>plan</u> your writing properly.

Warm-Up Questions

There are some tricky terms in this section but you need to know them all for your spoken language study. Have a go at these questions without looking at the answers. If you can't do one, read the section again and then have another go.

Warm-Up Questions

1) Give five features of real-life speech that make it different from written language.
2) What is the difference between an accent and a dialect?
3) Why do different groups of people use different language?
4) What is the name used for a person's unique way of speaking?
5) How is radio language different from TV language?
6) What is multi-modal language? Give an example of where it might be used.
7) Give three examples of the kind of data you might be given as part of your assessment.
8) Look at the labels on the transcript and answer the questions.
   a) This is Standard English — true or false?
   b) What does this symbol mean?
   c) What are these words called?
   d) What is this?

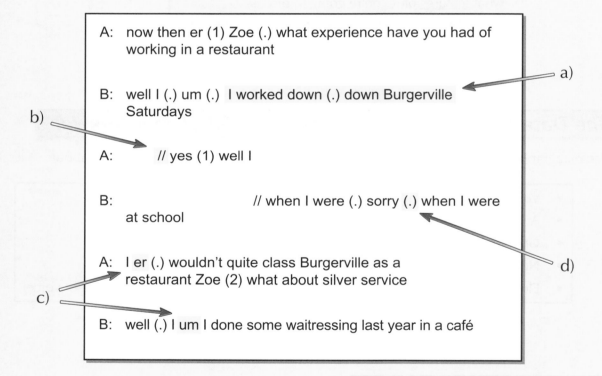

```
A:   now then er (1) Zoe (.) what experience have you had of
     working in a restaurant

                                                                    a)
B:   well I (.) um (.)  I worked down (.) down Burgerville
     Saturdays

b)
A:        // yes (1) well I


B:                            // when I were (.) sorry (.) when I were
     at school
                                                                    d)

A:   I er (.) wouldn't quite class Burgerville as a
     restaurant Zoe (2) what about silver service
c)
B:   well (.) I um I done some waitressing last year in a café
```

9) What three parts should your spoken language study be divided into?
10) What three things should you write about in the introduction to your study?

Speaking and Listening

You'll be assessed on <u>three</u> speaking tasks from three different <u>groups</u> — read on to find out more.

There are **Three Main Types** of task

The three <u>types of task</u> are:

1) <u>Individual presentation</u> — a talk in front of an audience. You'll answer questions afterwards.
2) <u>Discussion</u> — persuading people that your argument is right and listening to the other side.
3) <u>Role play</u> — playing a character and acting out a situation from their point of view.

<u>Teachers</u> are on the lookout for certain things in the speaking and listening <u>tasks</u>.
You've <u>got</u> to do these things if you want to get the marks:

- <u>Put across</u> your points <u>clearly</u> in a style <u>suitable</u> for the situation and audience.
- <u>Listen</u> to what other people say, ask <u>questions</u> and make sensible <u>comments</u>.
- Play the part of a <u>character</u> without slipping out of the role.

The **CAP Rule** stands for **C**ourtesy, **A**udience, **P**urpose

This is a really good <u>rule</u> to remember when doing your speaking and listening <u>tasks</u>:

1 **COURTESY**

Be <u>polite</u> at all times, especially when other people are doing their tasks.
If you're nice to them, they'll be on <u>your side</u> when you're speaking.

2 **AUDIENCE**

<u>Change</u> your speech to suit your audience. You have to keep people interested.

3 **PURPOSE**

Get your information across <u>clearly</u>. Keep your speech well-organised and to the point.

<u>REMEMBER</u>: CAP (Courtesy, Audience, Purpose)

Remember to make your points really clearly...

You should use <u>Standard English</u> for these tasks, unless you're playing a <u>character</u> who has a regional dialect. Just remember — CAP: <u>C</u>ourtesy, <u>A</u>udience, <u>P</u>urpose — and you'll be on track to do well.

Speaking and Listening

Speaking to an <u>audience</u> is different from <u>chatting</u> to your mates — here's what you need to know.

Use **Standard English**

1) Speak in <u>Standard English</u>. That <u>doesn't</u> mean you have to hide your accent — just speak clearly.

2) Don't use <u>slang</u>. You'll lose marks.

For more on Standard English, have a look at p.92.

Be **Clear**

1) Don't mumble. <u>Speak up</u> and look around the room while you're talking.

2) Make sure what you're saying has a <u>clear structure</u>, and isn't just a load of unconnected points.

3) Write <u>notes</u> to remind you of your <u>main points</u>, but <u>don't</u> write out every single word you want to say.

> Work out what your most important piece of information is. Think carefully about where you put it in your speech.

> Don't repeat yourself. Once you've made a point, move on.

> Choose your words carefully so they're suitable for your audience.

Listen Carefully and Be Polite

When other people are talking, you have to show you're <u>listening</u> and you <u>understand</u> what they're saying.

- <u>Don't interrupt</u> the speaker.
- <u>Ask questions</u> about what the speaker has said. If you don't understand something, politely ask them to <u>explain</u> it.
- When you give <u>feedback</u> on someone else's talk, mention the <u>good</u> things that they said.
- If you disagree with the speaker's opinion then <u>politely explain</u> why you think they're wrong.
- Only criticise <u>what</u> the speaker said, not <u>how</u> they said it — e.g. if they sounded nervous, don't mention it.

You must speak properly — don't use any slang...

You can be a bit <u>less formal</u> in a discussion, but when you're giving a <u>talk</u> you should only use <u>Standard English</u>. Don't use slang or dialect words unless you're playing a <u>character</u> in a role play.

Speaking and Listening — Individual Presentation

Three pages on the three different tasks you have to do — lucky you. First up, the presentation...

You have to do a Presentation

1) One of the three tasks is a presentation (on your own or in a group).
2) If you're allowed to choose your own topic, choose one that interests you.
3) At the end of your presentation you'll have to answer questions about it.
4) Your teacher can tell you more about your presentation and what it will involve.

This is the Type of Task you might be given

Here are some examples of the type of presentation you could do:

- Talk to your class about a subject you're interested in — e.g. one of your hobbies.
- You could be interviewed or you could interview someone else — e.g. you could talk to your grandparents about their childhood memories or be interviewed about your own.
- Make a case arguing for or against something that concerns you — e.g. club nights for under-18s, or more cycle routes in your town.
- Talk about a personal experience — e.g. a holiday or a concert.
- Make a speech to a large audience — e.g. in a school assembly.
- Listen to someone else's speech then present it in your own words — e.g. a politician on TV or someone at a school council meeting.

You can use slides, pictures, etc. to back up your points.

Plan your presentation

1) Plan your presentation in detail to make sure that it gets your point across clearly.

2) Think about who you're talking to — and how much they know about your subject.

3) Use Standard English, interesting language (see p.37) and a range of words to get good marks.

Your presentation must be suitable for your audience...

Your presentation might be given to the whole class, or to a small group. You'll find out who your audience is in advance, so you can make sure your talk is suitable for them.

Speaking and Listening — Discussion

For the discussion task you have to <u>listen</u> to other people and <u>get your own views across</u>.

One task is a Discussion with Other People

1) In a <u>discussion</u>, you have to <u>listen</u> to other people's <u>arguments</u> and try to <u>persuade</u> them that your point of view is right.
2) You need to think about <u>both sides</u> of the issue you're discussing.
3) When other people comment on what you say, <u>listen</u> to their <u>opinions</u> and <u>answer</u> their questions.
4) You need to <u>ask questions</u> as well. When someone else is talking, <u>pay attention</u> so you can <u>join in</u>.

Make sure you listen to others and ask questions as well as talking.

This is the Type of Task you might be given

Here are some <u>examples</u> of the type of discussion you could do:

• Discuss one of the texts you're studying — e.g. who's to blame for the deaths in Romeo and Juliet.

• Discuss a topic that affects you — e.g. whether your school should have more recycling bins.

• Try to solve a local issue — e.g. car parking in a busy part of town.

• With a partner, give a presentation to your class, then answer questions about it.

Back Up your Ideas to get Good Marks

1) <u>Think carefully</u> about the points you're making and make sure that you can <u>back them up</u>.
2) Give your own ideas and <u>encourage</u> others to <u>share</u> theirs.
3) Use <u>Standard English</u>, <u>interesting language</u> (see p.37) and a wide <u>range of words</u>.

During the discussion, remember to be considerate of others...

An important part of this task is <u>listening</u> to other people and showing you've <u>understood</u> what they've said by asking them <u>questions</u>. You also need to help keep the discussion moving.

Speaking and Listening — Role Play

The role play is a bit more <u>creative</u> — you have to play a <u>character</u>.

You get to do some Drama

1) For the <u>role play</u> task you have to play a <u>character</u> and present their <u>point of view</u>.
2) Role play is like <u>acting</u> — <u>imagine</u> you're the character and <u>act like them</u>.
3) You'll probably work in <u>pairs</u>, but for some tasks you might work in a <u>group</u> or on your <u>own</u>.
4) Your <u>teacher</u> will set you a task — it might be related to a <u>text</u> you're studying.
5) You're <u>not</u> allowed to use a <u>script</u>.

This is the Type of Task you might be given

Here are some <u>examples</u> of the type of role play you might have to do:

- <u>Explain</u> the actions of a <u>character</u> from one of the <u>texts</u> you've been studying — e.g. Jack talking about why he acted the way he did in 'Lord of the Flies'.
- Carry out an <u>interview</u> with a <u>character</u> from one of the texts you've been studying — e.g. a policeman interviewing Friar Lawrence in 'Romeo and Juliet'.
- Carry out an <u>interview</u> about an <u>important issue</u> — e.g. knife crime.
- Discuss a <u>current news item</u> as if you were a newsreader.

You have to Stay in Character to get Good Marks

1) You need to keep your role play <u>interesting</u> and <u>entertaining</u>.
2) Think about <u>how</u> your character would <u>act</u> as well as <u>what</u> they would say.
3) Think about the <u>situation</u>, and make sure your language is <u>appropriate</u>. For example, if you're playing a politician, you shouldn't use slang.
4) <u>Stay in character</u> all the way through.
5) Use <u>Standard English</u>, <u>interesting language</u> (see p.37) and a wide <u>range of words</u>.

Stay in character all the way through your role play...

You might be allowed <u>notes</u> or prompts for each of the three tasks, but remember that you're <u>not</u> allowed to write a <u>script</u> for the role play — even if you <u>memorise</u> it before you start.

Warm-Up Questions

Even though there won't be a written exam on this section, there's still a lot to learn. Make sure you can do these warm-up questions before you move on to the Practice Exams.

Warm-Up Questions

1) What three things are teachers looking for in speaking and listening tasks?

2) What are the three types of task you will have in your speaking and listening assessment?

3) a) What does each letter of CAP stand for in the CAP rule?
   b) Write a sentence explaining each part of CAP.

4) True or false:
   a) If you disagree with someone it's fine to interrupt and tell them.
   b) You should speak in Standard English in the discussion.
   c) It's best not to ask any questions in case you say something wrong.
   d) Your talk will be better if you try not to repeat yourself.
   e) It's important to try and look at the audience when you're speaking.
   f) It's best to write out everything you're going to say so you can read it out.
   g) It's ok to use slang if it is suitable for the character you're playing in a role play.

5) Why is it important to plan your presentation before the assessment?

6) Write a sentence explaining what you have to do in:
   a) the individual presentation,
   b) the discussion,
   c) the role play.

7) Give two examples of the types of task in:
   a) the individual presentation,
   b) the discussion,
   c) the role play.

8) Give two ways of getting really good marks in:
   a) the individual presentation,
   b) the discussion,
   c) the role play.

Practice Exam

Once you've been through all the questions in this book, you should feel pretty confident about your English exams. As final preparation, here are some <u>practice papers</u> to really get you set for the real thing. There are four papers — one for English Language and three for English Literature. These papers are designed to help you practice your exam skills — you won't actually have to do all four papers in your exams.

- Before you start, read through <u>all the instructions</u> and advice on the front of the paper.
- You'll need some paper to write your answers on.
- When you've finished, have a look at the answer section at the end of this book for some sample good points and answers to these questions.

General Certificate of Secondary Education

GCSE
English /
English Language

Paper 1

Surname
Other names
Candidate signature

Centre name				
Centre number				
Candidate number				

Time allowed: 2 hours 15 minutes

Instructions to candidates
- Write your answers in **black** ink or ball-point pen.
- Write your name and other details in the boxes above.
- Cross out any rough work that you do not want to be marked.
- You need to refer to the insert booklet for this exam.
- You should **not** use a dictionary.

Information for candidates
- The marks available are given in brackets at the end of each question.
- There are 80 marks available for this exam paper.
- You must use good English and clear presentation in your answers.
- Section A will test your reading skills and Section B will test your writing skills. There are 40 marks available for each section.
- You should spend about **one hour fifteen minutes** on Section A and **one hour** on Section B.

Section A: Reading

You should answer all questions in this section.

You should spend about one hour fifteen minutes on this section.

Read **Item 1**, the newspaper article called *Record Dragons' Den investment for Harry Potter-style magic wand* and answer the questions below.

1a   List 4 things the article tells you about the Kymera wand.

(4 marks)

1b   What do you learn from the article about how Duncan Bannatyne is involved in the project?

(4 marks)

Read **Item 2**, the article from *Hello* magazine about Jamie Oliver, and answer the question below.

2   What reasons can you find in the article for saying that Jamie Oliver is a successful chef and helps people and animals?

(8 marks)

Read **Item 3**, an extract called 'Local Customs' from a government guide called *Travel Safe*, and answer the question below.

3   How does the writer use language to inform and advise travellers about local customs?

(12 marks)

Now look again at all three items. They have each been presented in an interesting way.

4   Choose **two** of these items. Compare them using these headings:

- The layout of the text
- The use of pictures

(12 marks)

Section B: Writing

You should answer both questions in this section.

You should spend about one hour on this section.

---

5   Write a letter to a friend describing your favourite celebrity
     and explaining why you like this person.

                                                                        (16 marks)

6   You have been asked to make a speech to your local town council persuading
     them to improve road safety near your school. Your speech should include:

     •   what makes the road unsafe now

     •   how you think road safety could be improved

     •   why improving road safety near your school is important

                                                                        (24 marks)

General Certificate of Secondary Education

GCSE
English / English Language

Paper 1

Insert Booklet

The three items in this booklet are:

- **Item 1:** *Record Dragons' Den investment for Harry Potter-style magic wand,* an article from The Daily Telegraph

- **Item 2:** an article from *Hello* magazine about Jamie Oliver

- **Item 3:** an extract called 'Local Customs' from a government guide called *Travel Safe*

Item 1

Record Dragons' Den investment for Harry Potter-style magic wand

A Harry Potter-style wand that can change television channels with the flick of a wrist has attracted a record investment from Dragons' Den, the BBC2 show for entrepreneurs.

Laura Roberts
Wednesday, 25 August 2010
The Telegraph

Chris Barnardo with the Kymera Wand

Duncan Bannatyne invested £200,000 in the wand which can be customised to control a variety of household electronic appliances such as laptops, light switches, televisions, hi-fis, DVD players and even remote-controlled curtains.

The Kymera wand, a buttonless remote control, was invented by Chris Barnardo and Richard Blakesley who set up The Wand Company. The entrepreneurs* entered the Dragons' Den in a bid to get further investment for the product which can be tuned into 13 different devices and activated using different gestures.

Mr Barnardo and Mr Blakesley were offered a combined total of £900,000 by the Dragons for the 14-inch wand and accepted investment from Mr Bannatyne in return for 20 per cent of the business.

Mr Barnardo, 47, of Bishop's Stortford, Herts., said: "We planned our pitch very carefully and looked at the presentations of hundreds of previous entrants.

"We expected that we would be questioned strongly so we prepared our answers. When they all put their money in it was a real thrill.

"The whole thing was knee wobblingly scary and I'm not ashamed to admit that I was very nervous. It was terrifying when £900,000 was on the table.

"We are looking forward very much to working with Duncan because of his vast business experience."

The £49.95 Kymera Wand uses movement control technology similar to the Nintendo Wii, and can "learn" up to 13 infra-red codes from existing remotes and assign each command a gesture.

Owners will be able to turn up the volume by rotating the wand or change channel with a flick of the wrist.

Different moves can also be assigned to different gadgets, so the same wand can control a variety of devices.

The wand runs on two AAA batteries and enters a low-power "sleep mode" after 60 seconds of inactivity.

It uses a three-axis accelerometer* to detect movement, similar to technology in mobile phones where a picture turns to remain upright when the phone is rotated.

A tiny piece of silicon the size of a grain of sugar detects which way up the wand is and interprets its movements.

The inventors have already sold over 20,000 Kymera Wands since the launch in September last year and it is now on sale in 41 countries.

They expect to turnover £2 million in the next year with the help of Mr Bannatyne.

The Dragon said: "I see the magic wand rolling out very quickly over the next six months and I think it will do very, very well."

© Telegraph Media Group Limited 2010

*entrepreneur — someone who starts and runs their own business

*accelerometer — device that measures how fast something speeds up

Jamie Oliver

© Nils Jorgensen/Rex Features

Born on May 27, 1975, Jamie grew up above his parents' Essex pub *The Cricketers*, where he helped in the kitchens as a tot, and experimented with his mum's Aga cooker when she wasn't looking. It was an early training which was to prove useful when he left school at 16 to attend Westminster Catering College.

Jobs at several prestigious* restaurants in England and the rest of Europe followed. And by the time Pat Llewelyn, producer of the *Two Fat Ladies* TV cookery show contacted him after spotting him in a documentary about the *Riverside Café*, he had already risen to the level of sous-chef at the prestigious London eatery.

When the tousle-haired maestro stormed onto the TV cooking scene with his programme *The Naked Chef* critics were initially bemused by the 21-year-old's accent and presenting style. But they were soon forced to accept that audiences loved his simple, fun food, and good natured wide-boy persona.

The Essex-boy-done-great eventually caught the eye of British premier Tony Blair, who asked him to whip up an appropriately themed dinner for a meeting with the PM's Italian counterpart. The result was such a success the Labour leader offered Jamie the job of "food tsar" for Britain's hospitals, a role he declined.

He's a millionaire, was voted People magazine's sexiest chef, and is happily married to his childhood sweetheart. Life has been kind to celebrity cook Jamie Oliver.

Protective of his street cred image, *The Naked Chef* star has refused to endorse* international food and beverage giants whose product or marketing strategy do not meet with his approval. Both Nestle and Coca-Cola who asked him to pose naked for an ad campaign have been rebuffed. He does, however, have a promotional contract with pro-organic supermarket Sainsbury's.

Wanting to put his high-profile status to good use, the big-hearted chef opened a charity restaurant in London called Fifteen. As part of a TV show, called *Jamie's Kitchen*, he trained fifteen disadvantaged youngsters to work in the catering field. The show was a hit, and other Fifteen restaurants have been opened across the world, from Amsterdam to Melbourne.

Then in 2005 Jamie launched his hugely successful *Jamie's School Dinners* series, in which he campaigned to get healthier food on the menu in school canteens. Thanks to his efforts the government pledged to spend £280m on school dinners over the course of the next three years and Jamie was voted the year's most inspiring political figure at a high-profile awards ceremony.

Having overturned the school dinners industry the health conscious chef turned his attentions to highlighting the plight of battery-farmed chickens in the poultry industry. He launched *Jamie's Fowl Dinners*, and, following his exposé, supermarkets reported massive increases in the sales of organic and free-range chickens.

His personal life is just as successful. Jamie married ex-model Juliette "Jules" Norton whom he met while they were both still students at Newport Free Grammar school in a church just 200 metres from his parents' home. Key to the ceremony was a performance by an Elvis impersonator who sang *I Can't Help Falling In Love*. Jamie and Jules enjoy home life with their two daughters, Poppy Honey, born in March 2002, and Daisy Boo, born in April the following year.

*prestigious — well-known

*endorse — advertise

Item 3

LOCAL CUSTOMS

Meeting local people and getting to grips with a country's customs and culture is one of the delights of travel. Most of us know not to show the soles of our feet when in Thailand, but many a traveller has been left standing at the bar due to the mysterious art of tipping in American bars. On the other hand, you'll get a lot of cups of tea bought for you by strangers in the Middle East, and may never work out how to buy any back in return. Of course some

types of behaviour will be universally badly received — dressing inappropriately, loudly expressing political views and criticising your host country will never go down well. Good manners are always appreciated.

While local customs vary from country to country, the solution to any unwittingly delivered faux-pas* is a smile and a polite apology. Most people you'll meet will know you're not versed in local custom and be pleased to gently put you right.

5 unusual customs

•   In Russia and Central Asia vodka plays a part in most social rituals — expect many toasts and a headache in the morning.

•   In Madagascar it is considered *fady* (taboo) to point with an outstretched finger.

•   The popular Afghan sport of Buzkashi involves men on horseback battling for the carcass of a headless goat.

•   Land diving, an early form of bungee jumping, was invented on Vanuatu in the South Pacific where men hurl themselves off a platform with vines tied around their ankles — all in the name of ensuring a good yam harvest.

•   If you didn't know it already, you'll soon find out that ribbing Poms, normally about sport, is a national pastime for Australians and Kiwis!

Sometimes you'll encounter surprising behaviour from local people directed at you. In China, foreigners are greeted with cries of 'Longwai!'; in East Africa the cry is 'Mzungu' and in Thailand 'Farang'. The shouts are various terms to describe outsiders, foreigners and Europeans, and may follow you around on your visit to the country. While these shouts are normally accompanied by big smiles it can be a challenge to remain good humoured. The best strategy is to treat such comments as a mixture of a joke, and a gesture of recognition and curiosity — no harm is meant.

The best way to get in tune with the local customs is to immerse yourself* and expect your first few days to be something of a culture shock. Before you go you can get a handle on what to expect by reading guidebooks, chatting to other travellers and checking out FCO Travel Advice (0845 850 2829; www.fco.gov.uk). While it pays to be prepared, remember that discovering the richness of local cultures is one of the great joys of travel.

© 2006 Lonely Planet

*faux-pas — social mistake
*immerse yourself — get fully involved

General Certificate of Secondary Education

GCSE
English (Literature)

Surname	
Other names	
Candidate signature	

Paper 1

Centre name					
Centre number					
Candidate number					

Time allowed: 1 hour 30 minutes

Instructions to candidates
- Write your answers in **black** ink or ball-point pen.
- Write your name and other details in the boxes above.
- Cross out any rough work that you do not want to be marked.
- You will need to refer to an unannotated copy of the text you have been studying.
- You should **not** use a dictionary.

If you're doing WJEC, you can't take the texts into the exam – sorry!

Information for candidates
- The marks available are given in brackets at the end of each question.
- There are 60 marks available for this exam paper.
- You must use good English and clear presentation in your answers.
- You should spend about **45 minutes** on Section A and **45 minutes** on Section B.

Section A: Drama and Prose

Answer **one** question from this section on the text you have studied.

You should spend about 45 minutes on this section.

Harold Brighouse: *Hobson's Choice*

1   Answer part *(a)* **and** part *(b)*.

(a)   Read the extract on the next page. Then answer the following question:

What do you think about the way Maggie and Hobson speak and behave here?
Support your answer with quotes from the extract.

(10 marks)

(b)   Write about how the character of Willie Mossop changes in *Hobson's Choice*.
There are 4 marks available for correct spelling, punctuation and grammar in this question.

Think about:

- What Willie is like at the beginning of the play

- How the relationship between Willie and Maggie develops

- How Willie speaks and behaves at different points of the play.

(20 + 4 marks)

Harold Brighouse: *Hobson's Choice*

MAGGIE	Now tell me what it is you came about?
HOBSON	I'm in sore trouble, Maggie.
MAGGIE	(*rising and going towards the door*): Then I'll leave you with my husband to talk it over.
HOBSON	Eh?
MAGGIE	You'll not be wanting me. Women are only in your way.
HOBSON	(*rising*): Maggie, you're not going to desert me in the hour of my need, are you?
MAGGIE	Surely to goodness you don't want a woman to help you after all you've said! Will 'ull do his best, I make no doubt. (*She goes towards the door.*) Give me a call when you've finished, Will.
HOBSON	(*following her*): Maggie! It's private.
MAGGIE	Why, yes. I'm going and you can discuss it man to man with no fools of women about.
HOBSON	I tell you I've come to see you, not him. It's private from him.
MAGGIE	Private from Will? Nay, it isn't. Will's in the family and you've nowt to say to me that can't be said to him.
HOBSON	I've to tell you this with him there?
MAGGIE	Will and me's one.
WILLIE	Sit down, Mr Hobson.
MAGGIE	You call him father now.
WILLIE	(*astonished*): Do I?
HOBSON	Does he?
MAGGIE	He does. Sit down, Will.
	WILLIE sits right of table. MAGGIE stands at the head of the table. HOBSON sits on sofa.
MAGGIE	Now, if you're ready, father, we are. What's the matter.
HOBSON	That – (*producing the blue paper*) – that's the matter.
	MAGGIE accepts and passes it to Will and goes behind his chair. He is reading upside down. She bends over chair and turns it right way up.
MAGGIE	What is it, Will?
HOBSON	(*banging on table*): Ruin, Maggie that's what it is! Ruin and bankruptcy. Am I vicar's warden at St Philip's or am I not? Am I Hobson of Hobson's Boot Shop on Chapel Street, Salford? Am I a respectable ratepayer and the father of a family or –
MAGGIE	(*who has been reading over Will's shoulder*): It's an action for damages for trespass, I see.

J. B. Priestley: *An Inspector Calls*

2 Answer part *(a)* **and** part *(b)*.

(a) How is the Inspector presented in *An Inspector Calls*?

Remember to look at:
- How he acts and how other characters react to him
- The methods Priestley uses to portray the Inspector.

(10 marks)

(b) What ideas does Priestley explore about social class in *An Inspector Calls*?
There are 4 marks available for correct spelling, punctuation and grammar in this question.

Remember to look at:
- The ideas in the play
- The methods Priestley uses to explore these ideas.

(20 + 4 marks)

Joe Simpson: *Touching The Void*

EITHER

3   How does Simpson present Simon's decision to cut the rope after Joe's accident?
There are 4 marks available for correct spelling, punctuation and grammar in this question.

Write about:
- The events before and after Simon's decision to cut the rope
- The methods Simpson uses to present the decision.

(30 + 4 marks)

OR

4   How does the writer use the setting to give a sense of excitement and fear in the book?
There are 4 marks available for correct spelling, punctuation and grammar in this question.

Write about:
- What the setting is like
- The methods Simpson uses to give a sense of excitement and fear.

(30 + 4 marks)

William Golding: *Lord of the Flies*

EITHER

5   How is Piggy presented in *Lord of the Flies*?
There are 4 marks available for correct spelling, punctuation and grammar in this question.

Write about:
- what Piggy is like
- the methods Golding uses to describe Piggy.

(30 + 4 marks)

OR

6   How does Golding show the presence of evil in *Lord of the Flies*?
There are 4 marks available for correct spelling, punctuation and grammar in this question.

Write about:
- the effects of evil in the novel
- the methods Golding uses to present evil.

(30 + 4 marks)

Section B: Exploring Different Cultures

Answer **one** question from this section on the text you have studied.

You should spend about 45 minutes on this section.

Harper Lee: *To Kill A Mockingbird*

EITHER

7   Explain how Tom Robinson's trial could be seen as a turning point in the novel.
    There are 4 marks available for correct spelling, punctuation and grammar in this question.

   In your answer you should consider:
   • Important events before and after the trial
   • Attitudes to race
   • Society in 1930's Maycomb.

   (30 + 4 marks)

OR

8   What is the importance of family to the novel as a whole?
    There are 4 marks available for correct spelling, punctuation and grammar in this question.

   In your answer you should consider:
   • The different families in Maycomb
   • Why family is important
   • Family and society in 1930's Maycomb.

   (30 + 4 marks)

John Steinbeck: *Of Mice and Men*

9   Answer part *(a)* **and** part *(b)*.

   (a) Read the extract on the next page.
        How is the character of Slim portrayed in this extract?

   (10 marks)

   (b) How does Steinbeck structure the events of the novel so that they
        contribute to a mood of helplessness?
        There are 4 marks available for correct spelling, punctuation and grammar in this question.

   (20 + 4 marks)

John Steinbeck: *Of Mice and Men*

A tall man stood in the doorway. He held a crushed Stetson hat under his arm while he combed his long, black, damp hair straight back. Like the others he wore blue jeans and a short denim jacket. When he had finished combing his hair he moved into the room, and he moved with a majesty only achieved by royalty and master craftsmen. He was a jerkline skinner, the prince of the ranch, capable of driving ten, sixteen, even twenty mules with a single line to the leaders. He was capable of killing a fly on the wheeler's butt with a bull whip without touching the mule. There was a gravity in his manner and a quiet so profound that all talk stopped when he spoke. His authority was so great that his word was taken on any subject, be it politics or love. This was Slim, the jerkline skinner. His hatchet face was ageless. He might have been thirty-five or fifty. His ear heard more than was said to him, and his slow speech had overtones not of thought, but of understanding beyond thought. His hands, large and lean, were as delicate in their action as those of a temple dancer.

He smoothed out his crushed hat, creased it in the middle and put it on. He looked kindly at the two in the bunk house. 'It's brighter'n a bitch outside,' he said gently. 'Can't hardly see nothing in here. You the new guys?'

'Just come,' said George.

'Gonna buck barley?'

'That's what the boss says.'

Slim sat down on a box across the table from George. He studied the solitaire hand that was upside down to him. 'Hope you get on my team,' he said. His voice was very gentle. 'I gotta pair of punks on my team that don't know a barley bag from a blue ball. You guys ever bucked any barley?'

'Hell, yes,' said George. 'I ain't nothing to scream about, but that big bastard there can put up more grain alone than most pairs can.'

Lennie, who had been following the conversation back and forth with his eyes, smiled complacently at the compliment. Slim looked approvingly at George for having given the compliment. He leaned over the table and snapped the corner of a loose card. 'You guys travel around together?' His tone was friendly. It invited confidence without demanding it.

Roddy Doyle: *Paddy Clarke Ha Ha Ha*

EITHER

10 Read the extract on the next page. Then answer the following question:

Referring closely to the extract, show how Roddy Doyle creates anxiety and suspense in this extract.
There are 4 marks available for correct spelling, punctuation and grammar in this question.

(30 + 4 marks)

OR

11 Discuss how the character of Paddy changes and develops throughout the novel.
There are 4 marks available for correct spelling, punctuation and grammar in this question.

(30 + 4 marks)

Roddy Doyle: *Paddy Clarke Ha Ha Ha*

The first time I heard it I recognised it but I didn't know what it was. I knew the sound. It came from the kitchen. I was in the hall by myself. I was lying on my stomach. I was charging a Rolls-Royce into the skirting board. There was a chip in the paint and it was getting bigger every time. It made a great thump. My ma and da were talking.

Then I heard the smack. The talking stopped. I grabbed the Rolls-Royce away from the skirting board. The kitchen door whooshed open. Ma came out. She turned quick at the stairs so I didn't have to get out of her way, and went upstairs, going quicker towards the top.

I recognised it now. I knew what the smack had been, and the bedroom door closed.

Da was alone in the kitchen. He didn't come out. Deidre was crying in the pram; she'd woken up. The back door opened and closed. I heard Da's steps on the path. I heard him going from the back to the front. I saw his shape through the mountainy glass of the front door. The shape broke into just colours before he got to the gate and the colours disappeared. I couldn't tell which way he'd gone. I stayed where I was. Ma would come back down. Deidre was crying.

He'd hit her. Across the face; smack. I tried to imagine it. It didn't make sense. I'd heard it; he'd hit her. She'd come out of the kitchen, straight up to their bedroom.

Across the face.

*

I watched. I listened. I stayed in. I guarded her.

Nothing happened.

I didn't know what I'd do. If I was there he wouldn't do it again, that was all. I stayed awake. I listened. I went to the bathroom and put cold water on my pyjamas. To keep myself awake. To stop me from getting cozy and warm and slipping asleep. I left the door a bit open. I listened. Nothing happened.

General Certificate of Secondary Education

GCSE
English (Literature)

Surname
Other names
Candidate signature

Paper 2

Centre name					
Centre number					
Candidate number					

Time allowed: 1 hour 15 minutes

Instructions to candidates
- Write your answers in **black** ink or ball-point pen.
- Write your name and other details in the boxes above.
- Cross out any rough work that you do not want to be marked.
- You will need to refer to an unannotated copy of the anthology you have been studying.
- You should **not** use a dictionary.

Information for candidates
- The marks available are given in brackets at the end of each question.
- There are 54 marks available for this exam paper.
- You must use good English and clear presentation in your answers.
- You should spend about **45 minutes** on Section A and **30 minutes** on Section B.

Section A: Anthology

This section relates to the Poetry Anthology or set poet that you have studied.

Answer **one** question from this section on the poems you have studied.

You should spend about 45 minutes on this section.

AQA Poetry Anthology:

Characters and Voices

1   Compare the ways that voices are presented in *Singh Song!* and **one** other poem you have studied.

Remember to compare:

- the voices in the poems
- how the voices are presented.

(36 marks)

Place

2   Compare how places are presented in *A Vision* and **one** other poem you have studied.

Remember to compare:

- the kinds of places
- how the places are presented

(36 marks)

Conflict

3   Compare how conflict is presented in *The Right Word* and **one** other poem you have studied.

Remember to compare:

- the different causes of conflict
- how the different causes of conflict are presented

(36 marks)

Relationships

4   Compare how feelings towards another person are presented in *Nettles* and **one** other poem you have studied.

Remember to compare:

- the different feelings towards another person
- how the different feelings are presented

(36 marks)

OCR Contemporary Poetry:

Simon Armitage

5 What do you think is humorous and entertaining about the poem *Kid*?

Remember to refer closely to the words Armitage has chosen to use in this poem.

(36 marks)

Gillian Clarke

6 Explore the memories that Clarke brings to life in *Cold Knap Lake*.

Remember to refer closely to the words Clarke has chosen to use in this poem.

(36 marks)

Wendy Cope

7 Explore the ordinary and unexciting life that Cope describes in *Being Boring*.

Remember to refer closely to the words Cope has chosen to use in this poem.

(36 marks)

Carol-Ann Duffy

8 What do you find shocking and surprising about the poem *Stealing*?

Remember to refer closely to the words Duffy has chosen to use in this poem.

(36 marks)

Seamus Heaney

9 What do you find striking about Heaney's memories of his father in the poem *Digging*?

Remember to refer closely to the words Heaney has chosen to use in this poem.

(36 marks)

Benjamin Zephaniah

10 What powerful impressions of society does *Having a Word* convey to you?

Remember to refer closely to the words Zephaniah has chosen to use in this poem.

(36 marks)

Section B: Unseen Poetry

You should spend about 45 minutes on this section.

Pier

Speak to our muscles of a need for joy
  • W H Auden, "Sonnets from China" (XVII)

Left at the lodge and park, snout to America.

Strip to togs*, a shouldered towel, flip-flop over

the tarmac past the gangplanked rooted barge,

two upended rowboats and trawlers biding time*.

Nod to a fisherman propped on a bollard*,

exchange the weather, climb the final steps

up to the ridge. And then let fly. Push wide,

push up your knees so the blue nets hold you,

wide-open, that extra beat. Gulp cloud;

fling a jet-trail round your neck like a feather boa,

toss every bone and sinew to the plunge.

Enter the tide as if it were nothing,

really nothing, to do with you. Kick back.

Release your ankles from its coiled ropes;

slit water, drag it open, catch your breath.

Haul yourself up into August. Do it over,

raucously*. Head first. This time, shout.

Vona Groarke

Donegal

(for Ellie)

Ardent* on the beach at Rossnowlagh

on the last day of summer,

you ran through the shallows

throwing off shoes, and shirt and towel

like the seasons, the city's years,

all caught in my arms

as I ploughed on behind you, guardian still

of dry clothes, of this little heart

not quite thirteen,

breasting* the waves

and calling back to me

to join you, swimming in the Atlantic

on the last day of summer.

I saw a man in the shallows

with his hands full of clothes, full of

all the years,

and his daughter going

where he knew he could not follow.

Robin Robertson

OCR, Edexcel and AQA

11 Explain how Robin Robertson explores the relationship between father and daughter in *Donegal*.

Write about:
  • What is happening in the poem
  • The words and phrases in the poem
  • How the poet uses voice
  • How the poet has organised his ideas.

(36 marks)

WJEC

12 Write about *Pier* and *Donegal* and the effect both poems have on you. Write about how they are similar and how they are different.

(36 marks)

---

*togs — swimming costume   *bollard — a strong post   *Ardent — enthusiastic
*biding time — waiting   *raucously — rowdily   *breasting — rising over

CGP   Practice Exam Paper:
       GCSE English

General Certificate of Secondary Education

GCSE
English (Literature)

| Surname |
| Other names |
| Candidate signature |

Centre name					
Centre number					
Candidate number					

Paper 3

Time allowed: 1 hour 30 minutes

Instructions to candidates
- Write your answers in **black** ink or ball-point pen.
- Write your name and other details in the boxes above.
- Cross out any rough work that you do not want to be marked.
- You will need to refer to an unannotated copy 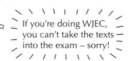 of the text you have been studying.
- You should **not** use a dictionary.

If you're doing WJEC, you can't take the texts into the exam – sorry!

Information for candidates
- The marks available are given in brackets at the end of each question.
- There are 54 marks available for this exam paper.
- You must use good English and clear presentation in your answers.
- You should spend about **45 minutes** on Section A and **45 minutes** on Section B.

Section A: Shakespeare

Answer **one** question from this section on the play you have studied.

You should spend about 45 minutes on this section.

William Shakespeare: *Much Ado About Nothing*

1   Read the extract on the opposite page. Then answer part *(a)* **and** part *(b)*.

(a) What impression would an audience get of Benedick and Beatrice here?
Look at the way both characters speak and behave.

(15 marks)

(b) How does Shakespeare present the relationship between Hero and Claudio?

Think about:
- how their relationship begins
- how their relationship changes.

(15 marks)

William Shakespeare: *Much Ado About Nothing*

BENEDICK:	If Signior Leonato be her father, she would not have his head on her shoulders for all Messina, as like him as she is. *[Don Pedro and Leonato talk aside]*
BEATRICE:	I wonder that you will still be talking, Signior Benedick: nobody marks you.
BENEDICK:	What, my dear Lady Disdain! Are you yet living?
BEATRICE:	Is it possible disdain should die while she hath such meet food to feed it as Signior Benedick? Courtesy itself must convert to disdain, if you come in her presence.
BENEDICK:	Then is courtesy a turncoat. But it is certain I am loved of all ladies, only you excepted; and I would I could find in my heart that I had not a hard heart, for truly I love none.
BEATRICE:	A dear happiness to women, they would else have been troubled with a pernicious suitor. I thank God and my cold blood, I am of your humour for that; I had rather hear my dog bark at a crow than a man swear he loves me.
BENEDICK:	God keep your ladyship still in that mind, so some gentleman or other shall scape a predestinate scratched face.
BEATRICE:	Scratching could not make it worse, and 'twere such a face as yours were.
BENEDICK:	Well, you are a rare parrot-teacher.
BEATRICE:	A bird of my tongue is better than a beast of yours.
BENEDICK:	I would my horse had the speed of your tongue, and so good a continuer. But keep your way, a God's name, I have done.
BEATRICE:	You always end with a jade's trick, I know you of old.

William Shakespeare: *Macbeth*

2 Answer part *(a)* **and** part *(b)*.

(a) How does Shakespeare show Lady Macbeth's thoughts and feelings in the extract below?

In your answer you should write about:
- what Lady Macbeth's thoughts and feelings are
- how Shakespeare shows these thoughts and feelings through the way he writes.

(15 marks)

(b) Write about Lady Macbeth's thoughts and feelings in a different part of the play.

(15 marks)

Lady Macbeth: Come, you Spirits
That tend on mortal thoughts, unsex me here,
And fill me, from crown to the toe, top-full
Of direst cruelty! make thick my blood,
Stop up th'access and passage to remorse;
That no compunctious visitings of Nature
Shake my fell purpose, nor keep peace between
Th'effect and it! Come to my woman's breasts,
And take my milk for gall, you murth'ring ministers,
Wherever in your sightless substances
You wait on Nature's mischief!

William Shakespeare: *Romeo and Juliet*

3 Answer part *(a)* **and** part *(b)*.

(a) How does Shakespeare make the extract below dramatic and interesting?
You should write about:
- the moods and attitudes in this extract
- how Shakespeare makes the extract dramatic and interesting by the way he writes.

(15 marks)

(b) Write about another part of the play that is dramatic and interesting.

(15 marks)

Romeo: Courage, man, the hurt cannot be much.

Mercutio: No, 'tis not so deep as a well, nor so wide as a
church door, but 'tis enough, 'twill serve. Ask for
me tomorrow and you shall find me a grave man.
I am peppered, I warrant, for this world. A plague
o' both your houses. Zounds, a dog, a rat, a mouse,
a cat, to scratch a man to death. A braggart, a
rogue, a villain, that fights by the book of arith-
metic — why the devil came you between us? I was
hurt under your arm.

Romeo: I thought it all for the best.

Mercutio: Help me into some house, Benvolio,
Or I shall faint. A plague o' both your houses,
They have made worms' meat of me.
I have it, and soundly too. Your houses!

Section B: Literary Heritage

Answer **one** question from this section on the text you have studied.

You should spend about 45 minutes on this section.

George Orwell: *Animal Farm*

4   Answer part *(a)* **and** part *(b)*.

  (a) What impression do you have of Napoleon at the beginning of the novel and later when he is more powerful?

  Remember to write about the society presented in the book.

  (12 marks)

  (b) How does Napoleon's relationship with the other animals change as he becomes more powerful?

  (12 marks)

Robert Louis Stevenson: *Dr Jekyll and Mr Hyde*

5   Read the extract on the next page and answer **all** of the following questions.

   (a) Outline the key events from the moment when Utterson writes a letter to Dr Jekyll in the previous chapter up to this extract.

                                                                     (4 marks)

   (b) How does the writer make the events in this extract seem horrifying and shocking? Use evidence from the extract to support your answer.

                                                                     (4 marks)

   (c) From the extract, what do you learn about the character of Mr Utterson? Use evidence from the extract to support your answer.

                                                                     (6 marks)

   (d) In the extract, Dr Jekyll behaves very strangely. Explain how Dr Jekyll behaves in one other part of the novel. Use quotations to support your answer.

                                                                   (10 marks)

Robert Louis Stevenson: *Dr Jekyll and Mr Hyde*

The court was very cool and a little damp, and full of premature twilight, although the sky, high up overhead, was still bright with sunset. The middle one of the three windows was halfway open; and sitting close beside it, taking the air with an infinite sadness of mien, like some disconsolate prisoner, Utterson saw Dr Jekyll.

'What! Jekyll!' he cried. 'I trust you are better.'

'I am very low, Utterson,' replied the doctor drearily, 'very low. It will not last long, thank God.'

'You stay too much indoors,' said the lawyer. 'You should be out, whipping up the circulation like Mr Enfield and me. (This is my cousin — Mr Enfield — Dr Jekyll.) Come now; get your hat and take a quick turn with us.'

'You are very good,' sighed the other. 'I should like to very much; but no, no, no, it is quite impossible; I dare not. But indeed, Utterson, I am very glad to see you; this is really a great pleasure; I would ask you and Mr Enfield up, but the place is really not fit.'

'Why, then,' said the lawyer, good-naturedly, 'the best thing we can do is to stay down here and speak with you from where we are.'

'That is just what I was about to venture to propose,' returned the doctor with a smile. But the words were hardly uttered, before the smile was struck out of his face and succeeded by an expression of such abject terror and despair, as froze the very blood of the two gentlemen below. They saw it but for a glimpse for the window was instantly thrust down; but that glimpse had been sufficient and they turned and left the court without a word. In silence, too, they traversed the bystreet; and it was not until they had come into a neighbouring thoroughfare, where even upon a Sunday there were still some stirrings of life, that Mr Utterson at last turned and looked at his companion. They were both pale; and there was an answering horror in their eyes.

'God forgive us, God forgive us,' said Mr Utterson.

But Mr Enfield only nodded his head very seriously, and walked on once more in silence.

William Golding: *Lord of the Flies*

EITHER

6   Read the passage in Chapter One from "They had guessed before that this was an island" to "They were lifted up: were friends."
    What impression do you get of the island in this extract?

    You should consider:
    •   The language that Golding uses to describe the island.
    •   The way the boys feel about the island.
    •   The way you feel about the island.

    (24 marks)

OR

7   What are your feelings about Ralph at the end of the story?
    Remember to support your ideas with evidence from the novel.

    (24 marks)

*ers are broken up into bullet points (•) to give
...ea of the type of points you could make in your
answer. These are only intended to give you an idea of
what you should be writing — there are many different
possible answers.*

Page 17 — Warm-Up Questions

1) False.

2) It's best to read the question before you read the text, so you know exactly what information you are looking for.

3) It helps you concentrate on what the question is asking for, so you can be sure your answer will stick to the point.

4) You can make it obvious by rephrasing the words of the question in your first sentence.

Page 17 — Exam Questions

1) Any four from:
   • Hutches/cages should be brought to a quiet room indoors or put into a garage or shed.
   • Small pets should be given extra bedding.
   • Hutches that can't be brought inside should be turned to face a wall or fence.
   • Aviaries or hutches should be covered with thick blankets or duvets to block out the sight and muffle the sound of fireworks.
   • Dogs and cats should be kept inside.
   • Dogs should be walked earlier in the day before the fireworks begin.
   • Windows and doors should be closed and catflaps blocked to stop pets getting out and to keep noise down.
   • TVs and radios should be switched on if pets are used to them to help block out the noise of the fireworks.
   • Dogs should be given ID tags. Pet owners should consider microchips in case their pets run away.
   • Owners should prepare dens for their pets so they have somewhere safe and comfortable to hide.

2) Answers should include at least four of the following points:
   • Fireworks cause many animals to suffer.
   • Some end up needing medication due to the stress caused by fireworks.

• Many animals run away from home during bonfire night.
• Animals have "acute hearing", so the loud noises caused by fireworks can cause them pain.
• Small pets are "easily frightened" by noises like fireworks.
• Small pets need "special care" when fireworks are let off.

3) Amazing experiences
• The article shows that Mike Perham had many amazing experiences. As the headline points out he became the "youngest person to sail round the world solo". This means that no one else had done it which is an amazing experience in itself.
• The article quotes him as saying at the end of his trip: "I am absolutely ecstatic. It feels amazing." This makes it seem that Mike Perham himself feels that the trip has been an amazing experience.
• He also describes experiences he will "never forget" such as "seeing hundreds of dolphins at once" which is something most people never get to see.
• He describes some of the beautiful things he saw, such as "incredible sunsets" which makes the experience sound amazing and worthwhile.
• The article ends with a quote from his father saying that Mike "is a very special son" and has done "incredibly well". This suggests that his father thinks that his son has done an amazing thing.

Difficult times
• Early in the article, the writer mentions some "euphemistic "Oh crikey!" moments". This suggests that there were many points when things went wrong.
• Even when things went right it seems that the journey itself was a difficult one. Mike Perham says in the article that the "ongoing low" was always being on his own.
• The writer uses the rule of three when describing what Mike Perham had to face on his voyage: "50ft waves, gale-force winds and a couple of hair-raising "knockdowns"". This makes the problems he faced seem difficult and relentless.
• The article also includes a description of "another drama" where Mike Perham had to make "30-second dives for 40 minutes in the Pacific". This shows how specific events were difficult and dangerous for him.
• The article includes examples of "horrendous" weather such as "50-knot winds" which shows that Mike Perham had to face extreme challenges.

4) See Worked Exam Answer on page 21

5)
- Item 1 uses pictures to make us feel sympathetic towards the animals. The cat on the front cover of the website article is buried in its bedding which makes it look as if it might be worried. The cat on the third page of the leaflet is staring out as if it is panicking.
- The picture of the cat on the third page also illustrates the point the leaflet makes about preparing a "den" for your pet, so it shows how owners can protect their animals.
- Item 3 uses a picture of a run-down building to show that the conditions Hector and his family live in are bad.
- The other photo shows some of the children in the family in their home. This shows the reader some of the people from the article and gives them an idea of the kind of conditions they live in.
- Both pictures in Item 3 show how bad conditions are and make the reader feel sympathy for Hector and his family, so the reader will be more likely to give money to the charity.
- The main title of Item 1 is "Fireworks and animals". This is informative as it sets out clearly what the main theme of the leaflet is. Putting these two things close together in one sentence grabs the reader's attention, as most people know that animals need to be kept away from fireworks.
- The main title of Item 3 is "When Danger Starts at Home". This is an attention-grabbing title because we normally think of "home" as being a safe place, but here it's made to seem a really dangerous place.
- The subtitles in Item 1 make it easier for readers to use the leaflet, as owners of small pets or dogs and cats are directed to the part of the leaflet that will help them.
- The subheading text under the main title in Item 3 makes it clear that the writer is asking for action on the part of the reader, as it says "Please help me". The word "please" makes the appeal sound more urgent, and the word "me" makes a personal appeal from the writer to the reader. The subtitle also shows that the money will help improve people's lives "for good". This means the reader is persuaded to donate, because their money will help provide long-term solutions to the problem, rather than a quick fix.

Page 38 — Warm-Up Questions

1) Language that appeals to our emotions - e.g. If we do not act now, many innocent little children will die of hunger.

2) b) is less interesting because there is no varied use of language or detail, and there is no attempt to build up any suspense.

3) A balanced argument

Page 40 — Exam Questions

1) *A good answer should:*
- be in the format of a letter
- use informal language like "you" and "my" as the letter is to a friend
- use descriptive language so that your friend can imagine the birthday you had
- be clearly structured so that your friend understands the order of events

Some points you could include in your answer:
- why you have decided to tell your friend about the memorable birthday (e.g. a really funny anecdote that you couldn't wait to tell your friend)
- why it was memorable
- whether you expected it to be memorable (e.g. you had planned an enormous party in Ibiza), or dull (e.g. you had made no plans and all your friends were busy)
- your reaction to the events of the day and what you drew from the experience, including positive or negative feelings
- use the five senses to make the writing more vivid/real

2) *A good answer should:*
- use language appropriate for talking to students at your school
- use informative language to make it clear where you did your work experience and what the order of events was
- use descriptive language and tell stories about what happened to make your explanation more interesting
- remember that an assembly is a formal situation

Some points you could include in your answer:
- why you chose this particular company for your work experience.
- how you set about getting in touch with the company to arrange your work experience, e.g. you wrote a letter
- details of the work experience, e.g. how long you worked there, position held, location
- how you felt before the first day, e.g. nervous or excited

- what your first impressions were and whether your colleagues were welcoming
- what the main challenges you faced during the work experience were, and how you overcame them
- what you drew from the experience, including positive or negative feelings

3) *A good answer should:*
- be written as if you're talking to teenagers
- use language suitable for a school newspaper
- explain why the charity needs their help and why this would be a good way to show their support
- give some quotes and facts to back up your argument — remember that you can make these up
Some points you could include in your answer:
- any perks e.g. goody bag at the end of the walk provided by sponsors, a T-shirt with the charity's logo on it and a day off school
- it would look great on their CV
- the walk would also provide a physical challenge, sense of achievement and would provide an opportunity to make new friends
- reasons why physical fitness is important, e.g. prevention of heart disease and weight loss
- which charity you are doing the sponsored walk for and why it is a worthy cause
- what the fund-raising target is for the group and what impact this money could have
- that the target could be reached more easily if more students joined the walk and got sponsorship
- details about the walk, e.g. distance, difficulty, and dates of event

4) *A good answer should:*
- be in the format of a letter, e.g. it could have an opening paragraph explaining why you are writing
- be respectful and formal as the letter is from a pupil to their school governors
- put across your view about the concept of free musical instrument lessons for all pupils
- persuade the governors to adopt your point of view by using persuasive language e.g. personal stories
Some points you could include in your answer:
- facts and statistics about the cost of providing free musical instrument lessons per pupil — remember you can make this up as long as it sounds reasonable
- whether most children would be likely to take advantage of the offer or not — if you want people to take you seriously, you could say you have done a survey to find this out

- your view about whether this would be a good use of school funds (e.g. a good use because of the benefits to students, such as increased confidence, or a waste of money and a distraction from studies)
- how you think learning a musical instrument compares to other possible activities at school, such as playing sport or taking part in a drama club, either positively or negatively
- what you feel the reaction of parents and students would be to your proposal

Page 52 — Warm-Up Questions

1) • Sentences a) and c) are more boring because they just make quite bland statements about Ali. Sentences b) and d) make the reader more curious because they hint at mysterious things that are not explained. This makes the reader want to read on and find out more.

2) Sight, sound, smell, taste, touch
- Sight: The sky was on fire with streaks of gold and pink, and we watched the sun set for a long time, grateful to be able to see it one last time.
- Sound: The shade given by the forest's trees was cool, and we could hear a thousand tiny insects chirping in the undergrowth, making a friendly humming noise.
- Smell: The strong, salty smell of the sea brought back so many memories of holidays at the seaside in Devon when I was younger.
- Taste: As soon as I swallowed, I knew that I'd made the worst mistake of my life. My throat was on fire, and all I could taste was the burning heat of chilli on my tongue.
- Touch: At first Jack was afraid, but once he put his hand onto the snake he realised that it wasn't cold and slimy at all. It was warm and smooth, like a leather jacket lying on a radiator.

3) • Peering through a thin slit between the window and the curtain, he glimpsed a ragged shadow. He yanked the curtain open. Tom screamed. He staggered backwards, shielding his eyes with his hands.

4) • The last line rounds off the plot and ties the whole piece of writing together. It's the last thing that the reader will read, so it needs to have a strong impact.

Page 54 — Exam Questions

1) • Last year, my life changed forever. My family moved from the countryside to the city. I'd only visited the city twice before, once to see the Christmas lights switched on and once to see a pantomime. My memories were of a massive, noisy

place bursting with people, so the thought of living there filled me with nerves. We spent endless weeks packing all our things into huge cardboard boxes until the house was completely empty. Fighting back tears, I said goodbye to my friends and promised to keep in touch. Then, as our car pulled out of the drive, I took one last look at the old house, the only place I'd ever called home.

The new house was a small blue rectangle in a long terrace. It had a strawberry-red front door and an untamed hedge outside. It took a week to unpack all of our boxes but, by the time we finished and all our familiar things were in place, I realised that the new house felt like home. Now, when I came home from school, the house looked awake and friendly, happy to have us living there.

Although I missed the open spaces of the country, I quickly started to enjoy the freedom that the city gave me. In the country it was difficult to get anywhere, because there were no buses, but in the city I could go exploring on my own. My newfound freedom made me more responsible and independent than I had been before, and I began to feel like a grown-up.

Emails flew back and forth between my old friends and I, and a few weeks after we moved they came to visit me. I was happy to be able to introduce them to my new friends — people I'd met when I joined an after-school basketball team. Once I got used to how busy, lively and noisy the city was, I liked it even more than the country. Moving helped me to grow up and it's given me twice as many friends as I had before. The next time my life changes, I won't be scared. I'll be excited!

2) • Five years ago, I moved to Poppleton High from my tiny primary school, where every face was familiar and I knew exactly what to expect. Despite all the reassuring words from my parents and teachers, when I woke up on my first day, I was terrified. What if I had no friends? What if I couldn't understand any of the lessons? My anxious thoughts turned to panic as I realised I was late! I leapt out of bed, threw on my scratchy new uniform and raced out of the front door to catch the bus.

As I left the house, I saw that the bus had already arrived at the stop. I hurdled the garden wall and sprinted down the road. As I ran, I noticed another person in the same uniform running beside me. We reached the open doors at the same time, clambered on board and slumped down on vacant seats next to each other. When we'd caught our breath, the boy told me that his name was Sam, and that it was his first day too. It felt so good to meet someone who really understood my nerves!

My relief didn't last for long. When we reached the school we realised that we weren't in the same class. I nervously entered my classroom and walked quickly to my seat through a sea of chat and laughter. As I sat down, the room fell silent. Looking up, I saw that the teacher had come in. Mr. Thornberry was a giant of a man. He had enormous glasses, a bushy ginger beard and was as bald as an egg. I caught my neighbour's eye and we both had to clap our hands over our mouths to stop ourselves from giggling. My fear that he'd catch us laughing was swiftly overcome by my delight that I'd made a friend.

The rest of the day passed in a blur of new faces, new subjects and trying to navigate our way round the maze-like building. By the time the jangling bell signalled the end of our final lesson, I was exhausted. The morning seemed like a lifetime ago, and I now knew that everyone else had been just as nervous as me. Whatever my second day brought, I knew I could handle it.

3) • Looking up from her computer game, Josephine realised that something was different. The light in her room looked clearer and brighter than it had a few minutes ago. Puzzled, she walked to the window and gasped. It was snowing! The roofs of the houses were already covered with a fine white powder, like a row of wedding cakes. She could see children running and laughing in the park, their parents huddled together nearby. A few metres away, a group of teenagers shrieked like five-year-olds as they lobbed snowballs at each other.

Pulling on an extra pair of socks, Josephine raced downstairs and dug her wellies, stripy woollen gloves and bright blue winter coat from the closet. Bundled up like a parcel, she was soon outside. She turned her face upwards and opened her mouth, letting the light, feathery flakes melt on her warm tongue. In the park, a huge snowball fight was underway. Scooping up a handful of loose, crunchy powder, Josephine pressed it into a ball and hurled it at the boy nearest her, scoring a direct hit on his chest. Laughing, he lost no time in getting his own back, and before long Josephine was cold and damp, but happy.

Hours later, as dusk fell like a curtain, Josephine finally decided it was time to go home. Her legs were heavy, and her nose and ears were tingling from the cold. As she went up the drive, she saw friendly lights glowing in the windows. The smell of roast chicken hit her as she stumbled through the door, exhausted, happy and suddenly starving. As she leaned against the radiator, warming her icy hands, Josephine was already planning the fun she would have in the snow tomorrow.

4) • I had never been so frightened. However, I knew that my safety depended on me staying calm, so I fought down the waves of panic and stumbled onwards, desperate to find my way home. A few hours before, I had set out to explore the rundown farm outside the village. People said that the farm was haunted and, since I loved scary films, I was desperate to see a ghost. Wandering around the lonely ruin, choked by nettles, I had lost track of time and found myself running for home as the last of the sun's rays faded. In the middle of nowhere and with no lights to guide me, I was completely lost.

After stumbling about in the dark, I eventually found a path and, thinking that it must lead somewhere, I followed it. Suddenly my foot caught on something and I fell face down on the muddy ground. From out of nowhere came a deep rumbling growl, and the ground began to tremble. A strange glow lit up the land and I realised, too late, that I was in trouble. Pressing myself further into the soft ground and trying to stifle my terrified sobs, I hoped I would not be discovered.

The noise got louder and louder until, in a flash of joy, I recognised it! It wasn't a ghost after all, it was a tractor! Scrambling to my feet, I picked my way towards its disappearing tail-lights and found myself on the main road, only minutes away from my house. I'd been going the right way all along.

Too relieved to feel embarrassed, I staggered into the warmth of my house. Coming out of the kitchen, my mum hugged me and asked with a smile, "See any ghosts, then?".

I felt my muscles relax as I recalled my silly mistake and giggled at the memory. "No mum, I didn't see a thing," I replied.

Page 73 — Warm-Up Questions

1) a) get the facts straight about the story.
d) quote relevant snippets to back up each point you make.

2) Answer a) is better because it refers to the audience.

3) a) Stage directions — description of the action on the stage.
b) Tragedy — a play concerning the downfall of the main character, usually as a result of a fatal character flaw.
c) Dialogue — conversation between two or more people in a play.
d) Soliloquy — when a character talks to him/herself but does it out loud so the audience can hear.

4) Poetic verse and blank verse both have a regular rhythm, but only poetic verse rhymes.

Page 75 — Exam Questions

1) • Friar Lawrence plays an important role in the tragedy of Romeo and Juliet. He agrees to marry them in secret. This is done even though he knows that Juliet is very young and is going against the wishes of her parents. He also urges Juliet to "take this vial" of potion so that she'll take on a "borrowed likeness of shrunk death" and the lovers can be together. Despite this, his plans are motivated by good intentions since he believes the marriage will "turn your households' rancour into pure love".

• However, Friar Lawrence is not solely to blame. In the prologue, Romeo and Juliet are described as "star-cross'd lovers", which shows that fate is an important force in the play. Several unlucky coincidences, such as the delay of the letter, are out of Friar Lawrence's control. Other characters must also take some responsibility. Capulet tells Juliet that he will "drag thee on a hurdle thither" to the church if she refuses to marry Paris. This threat makes Juliet feel that she has no option but to fake her own death, as her family won't be sympathetic.

• Romeo and Juliet are also responsible, because they make no attempt to control their strong emotions. For example, Romeo dramatically declares that he no longer fears "love-devouring death" as long as he has Juliet. Friar Lawrence then tells Romeo that "these violent delights have violent ends" and so advises him to "love moderately". This shows that Friar Lawrence tries to warn Romeo about his passionate behaviour, but Romeo ignores him.

• When Friar Lawrence discovers Romeo's dead body in the final scene, he blames "lamentable chance" for his death, which suggests that he believes it's due to fate. However, Friar Lawrence's cowardly behaviour could be seen to lead directly to Juliet's death. He leaves Juliet alone in the tomb because he "dare no longer stay" when the watch arrives. Without anyone to comfort or stop her, Juliet commits suicide.

• At the end of the play, Friar Lawrence accepts the blame and asks "let my old life / Be sacrificed". However, the Prince reminds the audience that "all are punished" in the end, as everyone is responsible in some way for their deaths.

2) • The play explores the conflict of good and evil through Macbeth's change from brave war hero to cruel tyrant. At the start, Macbeth is shown to be courageous and admired: Duncan proclaims "O valiant cousin! Worthy gentleman!" However, as soon as the witches greet him as "Macbeth, that shalt be king" he starts to consider killing the King. This shows that Macbeth's greed for power encourages him to be evil. This contrasts with Duncan's

goodness - Macbeth is corrupted by ambition, whereas King Duncan "hath borne his faculties so meek, hath been so clear in his great office".

• Although he considers murdering Duncan, the murder "yet is but fantastical" until Lady Macbeth taunts him "to be more than what you were" and persuades him to do it. He wants to "proceed no further in this business", which suggests he is hesitating because he knows it is wrong to kill someone. However, when Lady Macbeth calls him "a coward", he gives in. This suggests that he is weak rather than evil.

• Immediately after killing the king, Macbeth is "afraid to think what I have done". This guilt shows that, although he has done evil things, he is not a purely evil character because he regrets his actions. He also sees Banquo's ghost and begs him "never shake thy gory locks at me", which tells the audience that he feels troubled about murdering Banquo.

• Later on in the play, Macbeth murders Macduff's family, and shows no guilt for their deaths. This suggests that he gradually becomes more evil. Shakespeare presents this moral change with symbols of darkness and the unnatural. For example, after Duncan's death several unnatural things happen: "darkness does the face of Earth entomb" even in daytime, and horses go mad and "eat each other". As the play progresses, Macbeth becomes more surrounded by darkness and unnatural beings. For example, he goes in search of the "secret, black, and midnight hags" for another prophesy. This shows that he is seeking out evil and is no longer afraid of it.

3) • Beatrice is important as she sees how Eddie feels when he can't admit it to himself. She shows the audience that Eddie's feelings for Catherine are causing problems by arguing with Eddie about it, telling him to "get used to it, she's no baby no more". Beatrice also brings up the fact that she and Eddie aren't having sex anymore, which shows that she's not happy that their marriage is suffering and wants to improve their relationship.

• Having tried to reason with Eddie throughout the play, at the end Beatrice makes it clear that his love for Catherine will never be returned: "You want somethin' else, Eddie, and you can never have her!" Despite Eddie's treatment of her, she continues to stand by him until the end, which shows that she's willing to save their marriage. Eddie's dying words are "My B.!" which suggests that he still loves and values her.

• Catherine is important in the play as she is the cause of Eddie's problems. In the play she both fights against Eddie for her freedom, and wants his

affection and approval, for example she says that her relationship with Rodolpho "just seems wrong if he's against it so much". Beatrice warns her that she needs to act in a more grown up way: "you're a grown woman and you're in the same house with a grown man." She encourages Catherine to go out and meet other men and supports her decision to get a job and move out of the home. It shows that Beatrice sees that Catherine's increased independence would benefit herself and the situation with Eddie.

• In the end it is the relationship between Catherine and Rodolpho that brings the play to its unhappy end. Catherine knows that by choosing to be with Rodolpho she will "make a stranger" out of Eddie, because she is going against his wishes.

4) • At the beginning of the play, Othello and Desdemona are very much in love, although Desdemona's father, Brabantio, is unhappy about their marriage. He describes their relationship as "Against all rules of nature". By using this language, Shakespeare shows the audience that some people view their relationship as unnatural. In contrast, Othello calls Desdemona "my soul's joy," and says "I cannot speak enough of this content" at being with her. Desdemona calls him "My dear Othello." This affectionate language shows the audience that, despite other people's objections, Othello and Desdemona love each other.

• Act three, scene three is a turning point in their relationship. During this scene, Iago plants the false idea in Othello's mind that Desdemona is unfaithful to him, and he becomes suspicious of her. By the end of the scene, he says "All my fond love thus do I blow to heaven" because he feels he cannot love her any more. He even says "I'll tear her all to pieces!" which is the first sign of the violent end to their relationship. This scene shows how quickly Othello mistrusts Desdemona, believing Iago instead of his wife. Shakespeare is suggesting that their relationship isn't as strong as we first thought.

• In the final scene of Othello, the relationship between Othello and Desdemona has fallen apart. Desdemona maintains her innocence, and even blames herself for her own death. She still loves Othello, but cannot persuade him to trust her over Iago. Othello is torn between love for his wife and feeling that he must kill her. Shakespeare uses Othello's language to show us this confusion: he calls her a "whore" and a "strumpet", but also "sweet". When he finds out that she was honest, he is so ashamed that he kills himself. He loved Desdemona, "not wisely, but too well", which shows that his emotions were too strong — his intense jealousy destroyed their relationship.

Page 80 — Warm-Up Questions

1)   A verse.

2)   It will help you to work out what to write about.

3)   Alliteration is when consonants are repeated, usually at the beginning of words. Any reasonable example e.g. the green grass grew gradually.

Page 82 — Exam Questions

1)   • Shelley describes the statue's face as having a "wrinkled lip and sneer of cold command". This makes Ozymandias seem like a cruel leader, whose pride and power have made him unpleasant. This is emphasised by the word "sneer", which makes him seem arrogant.

• The alliteration of "cold command" makes it seem as if his ruling over his people was done without concern for them, and that he lacks personal warmth. This coldness is also emphasised by the fact that all that is left of him now is a "lifeless" statue.

• Ozymandias' pride is summed up by the message on the pedestal of his statue — "Look on my works, ye Mighty, and despair!" This shows how his pride made him arrogant, because he thought he was the most powerful king. However his proud statement is ironic as there is nothing left of his empire but "decay" and the "shatter'd" statue.

• Maybe Shelley is making a point about all people who take pride in being powerful, as the message on the pedestal is directly followed by the line "Nothing beside remains". This shows that, even though humans think their achievements are important, time is much more powerful and will destroy all man-made things. This is shown by the contrast between the broken statue and the desert which is "boundless" and survives more than the king's achievements which he boasted about.

2)   • Tennyson starts the poem with the phrase "Half a league, half a league, / Half a league onward." This means the poem has a driving rhythm from the start to create a fast pace like a battle charge. This suggests that Tennyson thought of war as exciting.

• Tennyson uses violent language to help the reader imagine the battle, for example "Sabring the gunners there". This shows that Tennyson wants to get across the idea that, although being a soldier is something that can lead to "glory", it is still a frightening experience. In the third and fourth stanzas, Tennyson uses alliteration, e.g. "shatter'd and sunder'd", to highlight how frightening the battle was and make it seem vivid to the reader.

• Tennyson shows his respect and admiration for those involved in war through his use of words like "glory". The poem ends with the reader being called to "Honour the Light Brigade, / Noble six hundred!" Language such as "Honour" and "Noble" suggests he thinks that it is important to remember the soldiers who were killed.

• The tragic side of war is shown in the lines where Tennyson says that, although the soldiers knew a mistake had been made, they were going to carry out the charge anyway: "Theirs not to reason why, / Theirs but to do and die". This shows that the soldiers were aware they would be killed but didn't turn back. Tennyson emphasizes their sense of duty through the strong rhyme and rhythm of the poem.

3)   • The narrator of this poem shows that he thinks romantic views about love, where the man admires the woman from afar, are silly. He does this by exaggerating those kind of romantic ideas until they seem ridiculous: "An hundred years should go to praise / Thine eyes, and on thy forehead gaze".

• He feels that there isn't time for him to sit and look at his mistress as he feels that death is creeping up on him: "at my back I always hear / Time's wingèd chariot hurrying near". This suggests that he thinks her fear of death will persuade her to sleep with him.

• He feels that they should act on their feelings of love by having sex. He makes this clear when he says that if they don't take their chance now, then the lady he loves will die with her "long preserved virginity" and that this would be a waste.

• The narrator uses imagery, like the simile "like amorous birds of prey" to describe how the lovers should act. This shows that his love for his mistress is strong and passionate.

• He suggests that love is something that can make life more exciting. At the end of the poem he says that though they cannot stop the sun from making time pass, they can "make him run". This suggests that their love will make time speed up, because they are making the most of their time together.

4)   • 'Below the Green Corrie' tells the story of the narrator's changing reaction to the mountains. The first time he sees them they seem threatening, but then he reveals that he finds them exciting. I preferred this poem because the way the narrator tells a story to describe his reaction makes it easy for me to relate to the experiences in the poem. 'Storm in the Black Forest' doesn't tell a story, instead it describes being in a forest during a storm without rain, and how beautiful and powerful the narrator

finds it. I found this more difficult to relate to because it is less personal.

• 'Below the Green Corrie' has the original and powerful image of the mountains being "like bandits" and "swashbuckling". This suggests how dangerous they are, but also how exciting and wild they seem to the narrator. These images make the mountains seem almost human, which makes the poem interesting for me to read. In contrast, the images in 'Storm in the Black Forest' separate man and nature by showing how wild nature is and how little control people in general have over it. Lawrence describes the lightning as a "white snake" which is "wriggling down the sky". This is a memorable image because it makes the storm seem alive.

• The main message of MacCaig's poem is that the mountains have added something to his life, in part because they are so dangerous. This personal aspect of the poem made it interesting for me to read. It gives a good sense of what the poet felt he took away from the experience: "They filled me with mountains and thunders." In contrast, the message of Lawrence's poem is that man's claim to be in control of electricity is made ridiculous by the thunderstorm. The final line, "supposed to!" mocks people who believe that nature can be controlled.

Page 87 — Warm-Up Questions

1) Yes you should, because it shows the examiner that you know how the book fits in with what was going on at the time, e.g. if it describes those times, or criticises them.

2) a) no.
   b) no.

3) Quoting to support your points is very important in any English Literature essay.

4) c) Write about how this extract fits in with the rest of the book, and why it's important.

Page 89 — Exam Questions

1) • Snowball is first described as "vivacious" and "inventive", which suggests he is an intelligent character. He believes strongly in the revolution, and is willing to fight bravely for it — the Battle of the Cowshed takes place with "Snowball at the head", which shows that he is brave and a leader. The character of Snowball shows similarities with Trotsky, a leader who helped command the Red Army in Russia when it was being invaded, because both Trotsky and Snowball led their troops to victory.

• However, he is not always a likeable character. For example, he doesn't care about the killing of humans, and tells Boxer that "the only good human being is a dead one". He can also be selfish, as he supports Napoleon's theft of the apples. Sometimes, Snowball appears to be too idealistic. He "conjured up pictures of fantastic machines which would do their work for them", which is unrealistic, and shows that Snowball's belief in Animalism means he doesn't always think sensibly.

• During the debates, Snowball usually "won over the majority by his brilliant speeches". However, it is noted that "Napoleon was better at canvassing support for himself in between times". Snowball is presented as being too idealistic about the ideals of the revolution, so he fails to realise the power of Napoleon's more practical tactics. Snowball is then completely unprepared when Napoleon uses violence to chase him off the farm.

• As soon as Snowball is gone, he becomes the scapegoat for everything that goes wrong. This happens gradually; at first he is simply "no better than a criminal", then an "enemy who has come in the night" until finally the idea of Snowball has become so changed in the animals' minds that he is "some kind of invisible influence, pervading the air about them and menacing them with all kinds of danger."

2) • Ralph is one of the main characters, and it is through him that the reader sees a significant change from order to chaos. At the start of the novel, Ralph creates order. For example, he uses the conch to gather the boys in an ordered group, and organises them to build a fire for a signal. The rest of the boys notice that he has a "stillness" that "marked him out" and soon elect him as chief. Ralph relies on the rules from his old life to create order, e.g. he says "We can't have everybody talking at once." The other boys are initially happy to accept some order, for instance the choir boys wear their black cloaks and caps despite the heat, because their uniform represents the security of their old lives.

• However, order begins to collapse, mainly because of Jack's influence. Jack encourages fear and violence among the boys. When the younger ones dream of a "beastie", Jack tells them "if there was a snake we'd hunt it and kill it". The threat of the beast makes the boys feel vulnerable, and Jack encourages them to become violent to protect themselves.

• Order collapses completely when Jack challenges Ralph and sets up a rival tribe. Jack's followers are often savage, and any remaining sense of order is lost. For example, when they kill Simon the scene is described as "no words, and no movement but the tearing of teeth and claws", and when the tribe murders Piggy, the boys are just "a solid mass of menace".

• Finally, Jack's tribe start to hunt Ralph, and as we see him escape through the forest he changes into a "screaming, snarling, bloody" prey. This image shows how Ralph has become a hunted animal, and is no longer a civilised, ordered boy.

• When the naval officer arrives at the end, we see the chaos from his viewpoint, and his expectations remind us how far from order the boys have gone. He looks at Ralph with "wary astonishment" and is shocked that they didn't "put up a better show". The realisation of how wild they all became overwhelms Ralph and he weeps "for the end of innocence, the darkness of man's heart".

3) • Throughout the novel, loneliness is shown to be unavoidable. George says that ranch workers are "the loneliest guys in the world" and there is little trust or kindness between them, so they find other ways to cope with loneliness.

• Candy has his old dog as a companion, although he doesn't express any strong affection for it. All he says is "I'm so used to him". He doesn't fight to keep the dog when Carlson wants to shoot him, which shows that he has given up on having lasting companionship.

• Crooks is ignored by the other ranch workers because of his race, and to cope with the loneliness "he kept his distance and demanded that other people kept theirs". However, when Lennie and Candy come into his room "it was difficult for Crooks to conceal his pleasure with anger". This shows that Crooks does want friends but is unfriendly to protect himself from being rejected.

• George and Lennie's friendship stands out in contrast to the loneliness of the other ranch workers. As Lennie says, everyone is lonely "but not us! An' why? Because... because I got you to look after me". George tells Slim he looks after Lennie because if ranch workers are alone "after a long time they get mean". George knows that when he is looking after Lennie he is kind and responsible, so their friendship makes him a better person.

• George and Lennie's shared dream of a place of their own also connects them. When they tell this to Candy and Crooks, both men are eventually persuaded to believe in it. The shared dream helps the men begin a kind of friendship.

• However, it is only ever a dream. When Lennie kills Curley's wife, the brief hope of the men joining together fails. There is no happy conclusion and the reader is left with the sense that loneliness is an unavoidable part of life.

4) • At the beginning, Joe calls Simon "an easy friend". Joe also appears to wish that he was more like Simon, saying that Simon was "everything I would like to have been". This shows the bond of trust between them.

• However, we also get the sense that Joe cares more about climbing than he does about Simon. When Simon gets frostbite Joe says "my anxiety seemed to have more to do with whether he would be able to carry on climbing when we got down rather than concern for his injuries". The tension between them also increases when they are in danger. We can see this from the words Joe uses to describe the way they "snapped" and "bristled" when they spoke to each other.

• After Joe breaks his leg, Simon's actions and words become matter-of-fact. Many of his sentences are fairly short, such as "He knew the score as well as I did." At first it seems as though Simon doesn't care about Joe's injury, but as Joe later points out, this is simply because "He had no time for sympathy".

• Although most of Simon's behaviour after Joe breaks his leg is quite cold, his affection for Joe is still clear when they are abseiling down the mountain and even after he cuts the rope. When they are abseiling, Joe describes the way Simon handles him as "almost tender". After he has cut the rope, Simon sees the crevasse and says "guilt and horror flooded through me" which emphasises his regret at cutting the rope, even though it was his only option.

• At the end of the book, the friendship between Joe and Simon is still strong and this is emphasised by the way Joe thanks him: "Thanks Simon … You did right". He also says that the experience they have shared has created "a deep abiding friendship".

Page 97 Warm-Up Questions

1) a) correct punctuation.
   c) paragraphs properly divided up.
   d) spelling all right.
   e) each sentence grammatical.

2) Standard English is formal English that doesn't include any text speak, slang or dialect words.

3) You definitely need to use Standard English in your GCSE exam.

4) • If you were writing a story with direct speech it would be OK to put the speech in non-standard English — so long as that suited the character speaking.

5) a) Give me those pens.
   b) Macbeth is a general who kills a king.
   c) The boy did as the teacher said.

6) Always start a sentence with a capital letter.

7) A full stop, a question mark or an exclamation mark

8) Separating the parts of a list, to break up a long sentence to make it clearer and to add extra information in the middle of a sentence.

9) a) The man, who still hadn't recovered from his cold, was feeling ill.
   b) I need to buy chicken, cherries, chocolate, cheese and chips.
   c) Why won't Robert's dog play with the children's dog?
   d) Sarah asked, "Has anyone seen Liz today?"
   e) "Does anyone want another cup of tea?" Andy asked, "because I'm having one."

10) This means, "I want to do an English exam."

11) a) Charlie's dogs were eating bananas.
    b) I don't like Frank's new trousers.
    c) Mum says it's going to rain today.

Page 104-105 Warm-Up Questions

1) a) affect.
   b) effects.

2) a) I wish I knew where I was going, but at least I know where I've been.
   b) If I were to have one wish, it would be that you were here.

3) a) I left my bicycle over there.
   b) The twins invited their friends to tea.
   c) They're the wrong chickens!

4) a) height
   b) athlete
   c) scene
   d) exercise

5) a) When I got home, I turned the television on.
   b) Today, I am happy.

6) a) When I get home, I will turn the television on.
   b) Tomorrow, I will be happy.

7) We began with a dish of lobster and crayfish which played against the flavours of the champagne like a kitten patting at a butterfly. The beef was perfectly roasted and so tender that I hardly needed to chew. The crème brulée was the perfect end to a delicious meal, with a silky texture and a diamond-hard crust. I left completely satisfied.

8) a) I go rollerblading occasionally.
   b) Evacuate the building immediately!
   c) Fruit and vegetables are extremely nutritious.

9) a) Katy's essay is much better than Claire's.
   b) Today was the hottest day of the year.
   c) Frank is the taller twin.

10) a) noun = horses, carriages
       verb = pulled
       adjective = enormous, heavy
       adverb = easily
    b) noun = Sonia, truth
       verb = wanted, know
       adjective = whole
       adverb = desperately
    c) noun = boys, headteacher, office
       verb = waited
       adjective = naughty, little
       adverb = nervously

11) Nellie loves those cream buns.

12) However, the book was written well, so I enjoyed it.

13) a) My sister's hamster has looked very happy since I brushed its coat.
    b) It's nice to see a smile on its little face.

14) a) I won't
    b) can't
    c) I'd
    d) it's
    e) they're

15) a) "I really need a holiday," said Martin.
    b) "Me too," agreed Chi, "I haven't been away for ages."
    c) "No," said Pete. "Not since that time you were nearly banned from France."

16) a)

17) a) quickly
    b) nervously
    c) loudly; blinding

18) The subject is plural but the verb is singular. It should say "The children only eat sausages."

19) —est

158

20) A simile says something is like something else. A metaphor says something is something else.
• Simile: e.g. Revising for GCSEs is like walking down an endless gravel road, barefoot, under a blazing sun.
• Metaphor: e.g. When you walk out of your last GCSE exam, you'll be in paradise.

21) a) Simile
b) Metaphor
c) Metaphor
d) Simile

22) • E.g. terrible, awful, dreadful.

Page 112 Warm-Up Questions

1) Any five from:
missing words
slurring words together
small talk
'vague' language
turn-taking
fillers
false starts
repetition
interruption/overlap.

2) An accent is how you say words, and a dialect is the actual words you use.

3) To give the group an identity and make its members feel like they fit in.

4) Idiolect

5) On the radio everything has to be explained with words. They don't pause very much because they have to fill the silence. TV language uses pictures, gestures and facial expressions to communicate, as well as sounds and voices.

6) A mix of written and spoken language. E.g. text speak, online conversations, emails.

7) Any three of the following:
transcripts of real-life talk
transcripts of audio clips
text messages or online chat conversations
scripted language
newspaper articles showing people's attitudes to spoken language

8) a) False
b) An interruption/an overlap
c) Fillers
d) A micropause

9) Introduction, data analysis, conclusion.

10) a) What kind of spoken language you're looking at.
b) What features you're going to discuss.
c) Where the data is from, e.g. TV interview.

Page 118 Warm-Up Questions

1) a) That you're putting across your points clearly and in a suitable style for your audience and the situation.
b) That you're listening to other people, asking questions and making sensible comments.
c) That you're playing your character without slipping out of the role.

2) Individual presentation, discussion, role play.

3) a) Courtesy, audience, purpose.
b) Courtesy: you've got to be polite to other people, especially when they're doing their tasks.
Audience: your speech must suit your audience and keep them interested.
Purpose: you need to get your information across very clearly.

4) a) False
b) True
c) False
d) True
e) True
f) False
g) True

5) Planning your presentation means you can make sure your points are as clear as possible.

6) a) Individual presentation: I will have to give a presentation on my own or in a group, and answer questions about it afterwards.
b) Discussion: I will have to take part in a discussion with other members of the group, listening to their ideas and trying to convince them that mine are right.
c) Role play: I will have to play the part of a character so the audience can see the character's point of view.

7) a) • talk to the class about an interest you have, or arguing for or against something
b) • giving a presentation in a pair and answering questions on it, or trying to solve a local issue

c) • explaining the actions of a character from a text you've studied, or pretending to interview a character from a text

8) a) • plan your presentation carefully to make sure you put your points across clearly, think about who you're talking to and how much they know about your topic

b) • think carefully about the points you're making and make sure you can back them up, use interesting language and a wide range of words to keep it interesting

c) • keep your role play interesting and entertaining, think about how your character would act as well as what they would say

English Language Paper 1 — Section A

1 a) *This question is testing your ability to select appropriate information from a text. So only write about the wand, and only write about stuff you can find out from the article.*

You will be given one mark for each of the following points, up to a total of 4 marks:

• The Kymera wand can control televisions, computers, light switches and many other electrical household appliances.

• The Kymera wand is a remote control without any buttons.

• Chris Barnardo and Richard Blakesley are the inventors of the wand.

• The wand can control up to 13 different appliances.

• The wand responds to different movements and gestures, which is how it activates different appliances.

• The wand uses technology similar to the Nintendo Wii.

• The wand costs £49.95.

• The wand allows you to change volume by rotating the wand, or change channel by flicking your wrist.

• The wand runs on two AAA batteries.

• The wand changes to a low-power "sleep mode" after 60 seconds of inactivity.

• It has a three-axis accelerometer, which is how it tells when it is being moved.

• A tiny piece of silicon detects which way up the wand is.

• The wand went on sale in September last year.

• Over 20,000 wands have been sold since it went on sale.

• The wand is being sold in 41 countries.

1 b) *This question is your chance to show that you've understood the article — read it carefully and only give answers that are relevant to the question. You could also back up your answers with quotes.*

You will be given one mark for each point you make about Duncan Bannatyne's involvement, up to a total of four marks. Your responses may include:

• Duncan Bannatyne has invested £200,000 in the wand.

• Duncan Bannatyne was asked to invest by the inventors of the wand because he is a judge on Dragons' Den.

• Duncan Bannatyne now owns 20% of the business, in return for his investment.

• The inventors look forward to Duncan Bannatyne being involved "because of his vast business experience".

• The inventors expect Duncan Bannatyne's help will increase next year's turnover to £2 million.

• Duncan Bannatyne is enthusiastic about the project and thinks it will "do very, very well".

2) *This question asks you about two things — Jamie Oliver as a successful chef and Jamie Oliver as someone who helps people and animals. Make sure you make the same number of points for each part, and back up your answers with quotes. You will get one mark for each of the following reasons, up to eight marks:*

Reasons for saying that Jamie Oliver is a successful chef:

• He has worked at "several prestigious restaurants" in England and Europe.

• He was a sous-chef at the Riverside Café.

• He is described as having "stormed onto the TV cooking scene".

• People loved his "simple, fun food".

• He was asked by Tony Blair to cook for the Italian prime minister.

• Tony Blair offered him a job as "food tsar".

• He opened his own chain of restaurants, which can be found "across the world".

Reasons for saying that Jamie Oliver helps people and animals:

• On his TV show Fifteen, he taught "fifteen disadvantaged youngsters" to become chefs.

• He campaigned to get healthier food for school dinners.

• As a result of Jamie Oliver's campaign to improve school dinners, the government pledged to spend £280 million on them over 3 years.

- He made a TV programme about the suffering of battery-farmed chickens, which caused "massive increases" in sales of free-range and organic chickens.
- He promotes Sainsbury's, which is a "pro-organic" supermarket.

3) *This question is different from the ones above — instead of finding information from the article, you should focus on the language. Look at how it is used to inform and advise the readers.*

Here are some points you could make about the extract — you'll get up to 12 marks for this question:

Language used to inform:

- When the article is informing the reader, the writer sounds confident, for example, "some types of behaviour will be universally badly received". This kind of language tells the reader that the writer knows about the subject matter.

- Within the main article, there are several lists of examples which inform the reader. Lists of examples back up the information given and make it seem believable. By telling us that in China tourists hear "cries of 'Longwai!'; in East Africa the cry is 'Mzungu' and in Thailand 'Farang'" the author confirms his point about "surprising behaviour".

- The language in the fact box is descriptive, for example the "many toasts and a headache in the morning" found in Russia and Central Asia, or men who "hurl themselves off a platform with vines tied around their ankles" in Vanuatu. These details make the facts vivid, to inform the reader about the customs of these places.

Language used to advise:

- When offering advice, the article uses phrases such as "the best strategy" and "the best way". These phrases make the advice sound like friendly suggestions.

- The reader is told "you can get a handle on what to expect by reading guidebooks". The phrase "get a handle on" is informal, so it sounds more like a friend's advice than a strict order.

- The writer also uses "you" and "us" throughout the article so it seems that the advice is aimed directly at the reader.

4) *This question asks you to choose two of the three items and compare them. This means you have to say how they're similar and how they're different. Two aspects are mentioned — the layout of the text and use of pictures. Don't forget to discuss both in your answer.*

You'll get a mark for each point up to 12 marks. Here are some points you could write about:

The layout of the text:

Dragons' Den

- It's a newspaper article, so it has a large, bold title.
- The title is also quite long — it gives a brief summary of the whole article, which means readers can tell at a glance what it is about.
- The paragraphs are very small and there is usually only one sentence in each paragraph. This means the article is broken up into easy-to-read chunks.
- The text is in columns so it is easy to read and clear.

Jamie Oliver

- It has a short title with just his name and no other information. This informs the reader about the subject of the article.
- A short summary of the article is given in big font in the middle of the text. This breaks up the block of text so it looks more appealing to readers. The summary gives the reader an idea of what the article is about, encouraging them to read on.

Local Customs

- It has a short title so you have to read more to find out exactly what the article is about.
- It's split into large paragraphs. Each paragraph gives an example of a problem and a solution, so there's a lot of information grouped together. This gives the impression that it is informative.
- The fact box is separated from the rest of the text and uses a coloured background. This is used to give extra information that's interesting to the reader. The fact box uses bullet points for the list of five entertaining examples. This makes them extremely easy to read.

The use of pictures:

Dragons' Den

- The photo's purpose is informative — it shows what the wand and its inventor looks like. It adds to the summary of the wand in the introduction.
- The photo makes the newspaper article look more interesting and colourful.

Jamie Oliver

• The photo's purpose is to show who Jamie Oliver is, so the reader knows who the profile is about.

• It is placed right at the beginning to back up the title.

Local Customs

• The photo is large and colourful, but it doesn't have a caption or relate to a particular point in the article. However, it shows a woman in traditional dress so it links to the general theme of the article which is local customs. This makes the reader think they might learn about some interesting local customs.

• Its purpose is both to make the article look interesting, so it is eye-catching, and to break up the text so the block of information looks more accessible.

Remember to compare the texts all the way through your answer and give reasons for you answers. For example, the newspaper article is laid out in small chunks that are quick to read and understand. This is because a newspaper appeals to people browsing and skim-reading. On the other hand, the Local Customs extract is aimed at people who are already interested in the subject of travel, so the text is large and more detailed.

English Language Paper 1 — Section B

5) *This question is an opportunity to be as imaginative as you want and to show off your descriptive language skills. The question is also testing your ability to 'explain', so make sure you explain why you like the celebrity in a clear and interesting way.*
A good answer should:

• be in the format of a letter — i.e. start with "dear" or "to" and end with "love from" or "sincerely"

• use informal language like "you" and "my", as the letter is to a friend

• use a variety of interesting descriptive language techniques to describe your celebrity e.g. imagery

Some points you could include in your answer:

• why you've chosen to write about this celebrity — e.g. you've just read an interesting article about them, or you'd like to buy tickets to their concert.

• your opinion about the celebrity — whether you admire them, would like their job, or think they're fashionable.

• some viewpoints about the celebrity that are different from yours, and why you disagree with them.

• some techniques that could be included when explaining — a quote from the celebrity, statistics (e.g. percentage of people who admire him/her) etc.

6) *This is a 'persuade' question, so remember to keep your audience in mind. Feel free to make up some statistics to prove that your suggestions would improve road safety.*
A good answer should:

• have the right form for a speech, e.g start by saying "Good morning Ladies and Gentleman"

• be respectful and formal as the speech is to the local council

• put across your view about the safety of the road at the moment

• persuade the council to improve the road by using techniques of persuasive language e.g. personal stories, rhetorical questions, lists, examples, quotations, examples of surveys, statistics

Some points you could include in your answer:

• The road doesn't have any traffic lights or zebra crossings to slow down traffic.

• The speed limit should be 20 mph, not 30 mph.

• There's no cycle path, so students have to cycle in the road.

• In addition to a safe crossing and cycle path, the pavements near to the school need to be widened. Children are more likely to walk or cycle to school, which is healthier and better for the environment.

• It is important that students feel the community respects them and is concerned for their safety.

• Drivers should set a good example, as many of the teenagers will soon be driving themselves.

English Literature Paper 1 — Section A

1 a) *This question is asking you to look at Maggie and Hobson's speech and behaviour and what this tells you about them. Don't forget to look at the stage directions as well as the dialogue. Here are a few good points you could make:*

• Hobson is asking Maggie for help, as he has been accused of trespassing. The way he speaks and behaves makes him seem quite desperate — for example, he repeats questions and exclamations when he says, "Ruin, Maggie that's what it is!" and "Am I vicar's warden at St Philip's or am I not?". His state of mind is emphasised by "banging on table" which shows how much he needs Maggie's help.

• In this extract, Hobson seems to rely on other people to show him how to behave, e.g. he gets up after Maggie does and follows her to the door. He only sits when Will tells him to. This makes him seem childish, so it reinforces how helpless he is.

• Maggie seems intelligent because she uses Hobson's views about women against him, for example when she says he can speak to Will "man to man with no fools of women about". By doing this she shows him that he was foolish to treat her so badly in the past. However, she is not unkind to Hobson, and eventually shows him that she still cares about him and will help him: "Now, if you're ready, father, we are."

• Maggie's words and behaviour make it clear that she is in charge of the situation and that she will only help Hobson on her own terms. This is shown on stage by the way Maggie "stands at the head of the table", to emphasise that she is in control. She also uses firm language when talking to Hobson, such as "you've nowt to say to me that can't be said to him".

b) *This question asks you to focus on the character of Willie Mossop. You'll need to show how his character changes by looking at his language, behaviour and relationship with Maggie. Remember to pick out plenty of quotes to support your answer and make sure you talk about different parts of the play, not just the beginning or the end. Here are a few good points you could make:*

• At the beginning of the play, Willie is described as "raw material of a charming man" which gives the audience a hint about what he will become at the end of the play. He is "not naturally stupid but stunted mentally", although some of the characters recognise his value from the start. Mrs Hepworth first recognises Willie's talent as a boot maker when she gives him her card and calls him "a treasure". Maggie also says that he is a "natural born genius at making boots". However, she also calls him "a natural born fool" because he is "loyal" to Hobson despite Hobson treating him badly.

• Willie doesn't put up a fight about marrying Maggie, even though he is already engaged. He just says, "Well, by gum! And you the master's daughter". He also admits to being nervous about being married in Act 3 when he says "I freely own I'm feeling awkward-like", but he changes after Maggie teaches him to read and speak in public, for example he speaks "loudly and boldly" later in Act 3 when Hobson visits.

• Willie develops feelings for Maggie and expresses his growing love for her at the end of the play when he says, "Thy pride is not in the same street, lass, with the pride I have in you" and kisses her affectionately.

• In Act 4 Willie is described as "prosperous" and having "self-confidence" but he is "not aggressive". When Maggie makes it clear that she will not come to look after Hobson without Willie's permission: "if Will tells me it's my duty I shall come", it shows that Willie has become Maggie's equal, in marriage as

well as business. This is such a big change that the other characters find it hard to accept. For example, Hobson's shock when he says, "But – but – you're Willie Mossop", shows how different Willie is at the end of the play to the way he was at the start. Willie himself is also shocked at his "own boldness" but knows that he is now "strong" and "confident".

(Remember, there are 4 marks available for correct spelling, punctuation and grammar.)

2 a) *With this question, don't just write down a load of facts about the Inspector – think about how he affects the other characters, and what his character represents. Don't be afraid to quote stage directions as well as speech - the Inspector's actions are important as well as what he says It's important to include the methods Priestly uses to portray the Inspector. Here are some points you could make:*

• From the start it is clear that the Inspector unsettles the other characters. The stage directions tell us that he has a "disconcerting habit of looking hard at the person" he's speaking to, and Mr Birling is "surprised" when the Inspector challenges him. The Inspector, on the other hand, remains calm, for example, when Gerald accuses the Inspector of "getting a bit heavy-handed" he calmly replies "possibly". As he can affect the others but doesn't allow them to affect him, the Inspector is immediately presented as powerful.

• Priestley presents the Inspector as a God-like character. He preaches about morals and justice and is often shown to be judging the Birling family's behaviour. For instance, in the Act Three stage direction "He looks from one to the other of them carefully". This shows the audience that the Inspector is weighing up the role of each character in Eva's death, and deciding who to blame. He also threatens to punish them with "fire and blood and anguish", just as God punishes sinners in Hell.

• The Inspector also seems to know everything about each character's past. Sheila highlights this when she says to Gerald "Why - you fool - he knows. Of course he knows. And I hate to think how much he knows that we don't know yet." The repetition of the word 'knows' and the way Sheila calls Gerald "you fool" shows how much the Inspector knows in comparison to the other characters.

• The Inspector is a mysterious character. At the end of the play, the audience still isn't sure who he was or how he knew the things he did. The fact that his identity is never revealed suggests it is not the Inspector who is important, but what he reveals about the other characters.

b) *You'll need to look at how each character is affected by their own social class, and the attitudes they have towards people of different classes. Think about how you feel about each character – if you dislike them, Priestley might be using them to criticise a certain attitude. There's a lot you could write about, so a clear plan will help you organise a good answer. Here are some points you could include:*

• In 'An Inspector Calls', Priestley explores the idea that attitudes to class can cause suffering and misery. The audience gradually learns the story of working-class Eva, and how each member of the upper-class Birling family has affected her life. Although the characters didn't deliberately set out to hurt Eva, each one is partly responsible for her suicide because of their attitude towards her social class.

• Priestley uses Mr and Mrs Birling to show typical upper-class prejudices towards the lower classes. Mr Birling fired Eva because he believed that "if you don't come down sharply on some of these people, they'd soon be asking for the earth". He calls the strikers "these people", which shows that he thinks they're different from him. The phrase "asking for the earth" shows he assumes they're greedy, even though they only asked for a small pay rise. Mrs Birling doesn't bother finding out if Eva truly deserves her charity because she immediately dismisses her as a "girl of that sort". They both make assumptions, which means Eva is treated unfairly.

• Priestley uses irony to make fun of the upper classes. For example, Mrs Birling believes lower-class people don't have morals, but her own son is an alcoholic who sleeps with prostitutes and steals money. She is completely unaware of how ridiculous her viewpoint is, which makes her seem even more ridiculous to the audience.

• The Inspector provides a contrast to the Birlings because he doesn't think class is important - for example, he isn't impressed when Mr Birling tells him that the Chief Constable is "an old friend of mine".

• The Inspector also shows that he believes in fairness and equality when he says "We are members of one body. We are responsible for each other." This is the main idea in the play, and the Inspector uses a lot of emotional language and images to show how important it is to be kind to others. For example, he says people will suffer "fire and blood and anguish" if they don't learn to look after people like Eva, who was "alone, friendless, almost penniless, desperate".

(Remember, there are 4 marks available for correct spelling, punctuation and grammar.)

3) *You'll need to write about the part of the book when Simon cuts the rope, as well as what happens before and after this point in the book. Here are a few good points you could make:*

• The tension builds through the chapter, "The Final Choice", up to the moment when Simon cuts the rope. Simpson creates this tension by describing how they keep losing and gaining control of the situation. For example, he says "We had regained control" and describes a "sense of optimism" just before he goes over the ice cliff. This makes the disaster seem even more shocking, and this is highlighted by the use of tense, panicked language such as "frantic warning".

• Before the rope is cut, the narration switches to Simon's point of view. This means that the reader is able to relate to his situation. We have access to Simon's thoughts and can see how difficult the act of cutting the rope is for him.

• The narrative quickly moves from getting the knife to cutting the rope. The act of making the decision to cut the rope is not narrated. Simon only says, "I had already made the decision". He also says that the thought of cutting the rope "came out of nowhere", making it seem as if someone else made the decision.

• Simon's confusion after cutting the rope shows how difficult cutting the rope actually was. He is torn between feeling "pleased" and confused that he doesn't yet feel guilty. It is only later that he says "guilt and horror flooded through me".

• When Joe discovers the frayed end of rope, he says "I had known all along" which suggests that he feels that Simon did the right thing. This is confirmed at the end of the book when Joe tells Simon, "I don't blame you. You had no choice" which shows that he understands Simon's decision.

(Remember, there are 4 marks available for correct spelling, punctuation and grammar.)

4) *This question asks you to think about the dramatic setting of the book and the way Simpson describes it. Get plenty of quotes into your answer and explain how they show excitement or fear. Here are a few good points you could make:*

• At the beginning of the book, Joe describes his surroundings with excitement. He describes "the most spectacular ring of ice mountains I had ever seen". This shows the impression the mountains have on him even before he starts climbing. He also compares two of the peaks to "extravagant castles of icing sugar" which makes the setting seem like an unreal fantasy.

• As Simon and Joe begin their climb, they see Siula Grande and Joe says he was "a little awed" by the sight of it. The word "awed" suggests both excitement and fear and shows how impressive the mountain was. He also uses words like "huge" and "astonishing" to show the scale of the mountains.

• As the conditions get worse, Joe says the mountain had "lost its excitement". Words such as "yawning abyss" make the mountains seem alive and more threatening, as if they could actually kill the men.

• Joe describes the crevasse as having "the feel of tombs". He associates it with death because he believes he will die there. He also uses personification to describe the crevasse, "as if this thing had waited for a victim". This makes Joe seem small and helpless in comparison.

• As Simon comes down the mountain alone, he describes the mountains as "perfect" but now they leave him feeling "empty". Simon also uses personification when he says, "It was as if the mountains were holding their breath, waiting for another death." At this point the mountains seem threatening, as if they are waiting to watch him die.

(Remember, there are 4 marks available for correct spelling, punctuation and grammar.)

5) *For this question you'll need to think about the things Piggy does in the book, the way that Golding describes him, and the way the other characters act towards him. Here are some things you could say:*

• Piggy is at first described in the book as "the fat boy". The fact that he is overweight, has glasses and is asthmatic is repeatedly commented on during the novel. This makes some of the other boys, like Jack, pick him out as a victim to be bullied.

• Golding uses Piggy's glasses to symbolise that he is vulnerable and different from the other boys. When his glasses are smashed this is an example of bullying. Although he is represented as physically weak his strength of character comes through against all these odds.

• Piggy is less posh than the other boys, which makes them see him as different. Golding shows this in the way Piggy speaks; "We was scared".

• Piggy is the character who is most concerned with sticking to the rules that the boys have made. He reminds the other characters that they are only supposed to speak at their gatherings when they have the conch. This shows that, of all the characters, he is the one who most wants to behave like an adult, and who misses the ordered world of adults. His longing for the presence of adults is also shown in the way he often talks about what his auntie has said.

• Piggy is portrayed as one of the most intelligent characters. Golding makes Ralph recognise this: "… Piggy, for all his ludicrous body, had brains." But it is also clear that being intelligent isn't enough to make Piggy a leader, and it doesn't help him to survive.

• Piggy is one of the characters the reader most looks up to in 'Lord of the Flies'. Both the reader and Ralph admire him for his loyalty, as he sticks by Ralph even when things are going badly. In the end, however, this loyalty is one of the things which leads to him getting killed: he's murdered as he tries to convince everyone that they should be sensible like Ralph.

(Remember, there are 4 marks available for correct spelling, punctuation and grammar.)

6) *This kind of theme question comes up a lot in the exams. Think about all the things that happen in the novel which could be described as evil, and how Golding makes it clear that evil is a force on the island. Here are some things you could say:*

• Evil is an important theme in 'Lord of the Flies'. The novel describes how the characters stuck on the island change from schoolboys into savages, and by the end a number of characters have been murdered.

• The novel takes place against the background of war, which shows that evil is going on in the wider world.

• The 'littluns' are all frightened of the Beast, a terrible creature they imagine is out to hurt them. To start with, most of the bigger boys mock the idea of a Beast, but by the end of the novel almost all the boys believe in it.

• Jack becomes more and more evil as the novel progresses. He feels cheated when he doesn't get made chief, and takes out a lot of his anger on Piggy. He becomes obsessed with hunting. Golding writes that he feels "a compulsion to track down and kill".

• Roger is the character who is most clearly evil in the book. Golding shows how he is someone who is likely to turn bad early in the novel, when he starts throwing stones at one of the 'littluns', but "threw to miss".

• Simon says that he thinks the beast is "only us", and later in the book, the 'Lord of the Flies' — the pig's head on a stick — says to Simon: "'Fancy thinking the Beast was something you could hunt and kill! … You knew didn't you? I'm part of you?". This shows that Simon recognises that the evil isn't something out on the island, but something within the boys themselves.

• Golding shows how Ralph learns the truth about evil, that it isn't something 'out there' to be scared of in a childish way, but something in people themselves. At the end of the novel, he cries for "the darkness of man's heart".

(Remember, there are 4 marks available for correct spelling, punctuation and grammar.)

English Literature Paper 1 — Section B

7) *The bullet points are part of the question, so don't just skim over them – they're there to help you include the right things in your answer. Use the bullet points to help organise and plan your answer. It's really important that you link your answer to society at the time the novel was written – the examiners will be looking out for it. Here are a few good points you could make in your answer:*

• Most of the people in Maycomb are shown in a mainly positive light until the trial, when their true prejudices are made clear. For example, Atticus is threatened by a mob, and one of the men in the courtroom criticises Atticus before the trial by saying "Atticus aims to defend him. That's what I don't like about it." Atticus says that racism is Maycomb's "usual disease" which shows how deep prejudices were in 1930's America — it was "usual" for people to be racist.

• Before the trial, Jem and Scout spend their time playing childish Boo Radley games. The trial forces them to grow up and enter the adult world. They play fewer games as the trial approaches and Scout asks Atticus what rape is. Jem's innocent belief that Atticus will win the trial is shown when he says to Reverend Sykes, "don't fret, we've won it". This contrasts with his shock after the trial when he cries and repeats "It ain't right". After the trial, he starts to behave in a more grown-up way.

• Despite the verdict, the trial marks the beginning of a slow change in attitudes in Maycomb. The fact that Atticus, Maycomb's most respected lawyer, was chosen to defend a black man shows that Tom Robinson was given the best chance of being found innocent. The jury takes several hours to reach its verdict, which was unusual in a case involving a black man at that time. Miss Maudie says that this is a "baby step" towards a less racist society, because people are starting to overcome their prejudices.

(Remember, there are 4 marks available for correct spelling, punctuation and grammar.)

8) *There are lots of different ways of answering this question so make a quick plan before you start writing your answer. That way you'll be able to organise your thoughts and your answer will have a clear structure. Here are a few good points you could make in your answer:*

• Family is important in the novel because it affects a person's place in society. The people of Maycomb judge each other according to which family they are from — it's another kind of prejudice. Aunt Alexandra bans Scout from playing with Walter Cunningham because "he – is – trash… I'll not have you around him, picking up his habits and learning

Lord-knows-what". Her view of Walter is based on her opinion of the Cunningham family as a whole.

• Like many families in Maycomb, the Finch family history is also tied in to the history of the South. Scout mentions that they're Southerners on the first page of the novel and that their ancestors owned slaves. Having a long family history in the South is a source of pride for many people in Maycomb, but it also means that many of the town's prejudices have passed from generation to generation and are difficult to change.

• The novel also explores how children learn morals from their family. Atticus spends time teaching Jem and Scout about the world, which contrasts with Bob Ewell's neglect of his children. Scout overhears Atticus say to Uncle Jack, "When a child asks you something, answer him" which shows that Atticus believes that parents should be honest with their children. He gives his children a good moral education by teaching them to respect other people. Atticus tells Scout to imagine herself in someone else's skin so she can "walk around in it" and understand people better.

(Remember, there are 4 marks available for correct spelling, punctuation and grammar.)

9) a) *You'll need to back up your ideas with examples from the extract. You can talk about things that aren't in the extract too, as long as they're relevant to the question. Here are some things you could say:*

• Steinbeck first describes Slim standing in the doorway to the bunkhouse wearing jeans and a jacket, "Like the others". In contrast to this image, Slim moves into the room "with a majesty only achieved by royalty and master craftsmen". This shows us that Slim is both similar to and different from the rest of the men on the ranch.

• Slim's job on the ranch is important — his job title "jerkline skinner" is emphasised through repetition. Steinbeck also writes that Slim can drive "ten, sixteen, even twenty mules" which highlights his skill.

• The next paragraph presents Slim as down-to-earth. His first words to George and Lennie are "It's brighter'n a bitch outside" which is something that any of the men on the ranch might say. Although Slim fits in with the others, he is also separate from them and they look to him for advice, for example, he makes the final decision about whether Candy's dog should be put down.

• Although Slim is powerful, he treats others well. He welcomes George and Lennie with warmth when he says "Hope you get on my team". This is very different from many of the other men in the novel. His kindness and generosity are also shown later in the novel, for example when he gives Lennie the puppy and when he looks after Curley after his hand is crushed, despite the fact that Curley has just accused Slim of trying to seduce his wife.

• Almost immediately, we realise that Slim approves of the friendship between George and Lennie and will be on George and Lennie's side later in the story. When he talks to them, his voice is "very gentle" which shows that he is kind and friendly. This contrasts with the way that other men on the ranch speak, such as Carlson. At the end of the novel, Slim seems to understand that George had to kill Lennie, and that he shot him out of love and friendship. In this way, Slim again shows that he understands the relationship between George and Lennie.

9) b) *Don't be put off by the word 'structure' in this question — it basically means that you need to look at the order of events in the novel and say how they affect the mood. Don't fall into the trap of just describing the plot. Here's some things you could say:*

• The novel is circular — it begins and ends with George and Lennie standing by the same river. On both occasions, Lennie has done something wrong and the two friends have been forced to run away. This sets up the idea that the characters are helpless to change anything about their lives.

• Events that happen later in the novel mirror earlier ones. The girl who Lennie grabbed in Weed was wearing a red dress. When she struggled and cried out, Lennie held on harder. Later, Curley's wife (who always wears red) ends up in a similar situation with Lennie and he kills her.

• George sees straight away that Curley's wife is going to be trouble and warns Lennie to stay away from her — "You leave her be". He also knows that Curley will cause them problems. Immediately after their first meeting with Curley, George reminds Lennie about what to do if he gets into "any kind of trouble". Steinbeck is setting the scene for what happens later on.

• When Lennie kills Curley's wife, he's gone too far. George can't do anything to save him this time — he has no choice but to shoot Lennie or see him get lynched by Curley and the other men. He can't let this happen to his friend. George is completely helpless.

• Events keep repeating themselves, but they get worse each time. For example, Lennie first kills a mouse, then the puppy, and finally Curley's wife. This makes the reader feel that the outcome is inevitable.

• The chapters which begin with characters thinking about the dream always end with someone ruining the mood of the scene. For example, in Chapter 4, Candy tells Crooks about the dream of having their own farm and Crooks begins to be tempted by the dream.

However, at the end of the scene, he rejects it again, saying "I wouldn' want to go no place like that." This shows that not even the individual chapters end happily, suggesting that the book will have an unhappy ending.

(Remember, there are 4 marks available for correct spelling, punctuation and grammar.)

10) *With a question like this, you need to avoid just describing the events in the extract. You're being asked to write about the mood that Roddy Doyle has created, so look carefully at his style. Here are some things you could say:*

• In this passage, the level of suspense varies depending on who understands what is happening. The suspense is greatest when neither Paddy nor the reader knows what is happening, as in the first sentence, "I recognised it but I didn't know what it was." It decreases when both the reader and Paddy know what has happened, for example when Paddy says, "He'd hit her."

• In the second paragraph, the sound is further described as a "smack". The word "smack" is angry and suggests pain, so it is linked to danger. The reader's anxiety increases here because we suspect what has happened, but still do not know for certain.

• Paddy, Ma and Deidre seem panicked. Words like "whooshed" and the repetition of "quick" and "going quicker" suggest that Ma is trying to escape something, although the narrator is unsure of what this is. The use of short sentences creates drama, because the descriptions come in sharp bursts and everything happens quickly.

• The level of suspense drops in the third paragraph, as the narrator realises what has happened. However, the tension builds again in the final paragraph, as Paddy waits for something else to happen. The short sentences, "I watched. I listened. I stayed in." make it sound almost as though Paddy is holding his breath, waiting for Da to return. The repetition of "Nothing happened" creates a sense of silence and suspense, as the reader and Paddy wait for something to break the tension.

(Remember, there are 4 marks available for correct spelling, punctuation and grammar.)

11) *The key words in this question are 'changes' and 'develops', so you need to explain what Paddy's like at the beginning, why he changes and how he's different by the end. Before you start writing, make a plan and jot down some examples or quotes that will back up your points. Here are some points you could include:*

• Early in the novel, Paddy sees his parents fighting and doesn't understand what's happening. He only knows that "something had happened; something". As the book progresses, he becomes more aware of the tension in the house. He learns that he can control this tension by being deliberately funny and distracting.

• Paddy tries to protect his family from arguments and begins to blame his father for the tension within the family. When he talks about an argument he had with Da he says, "I'd beaten da. It had been easy". This shows that he's becoming aware of his father's flaws and his own power.

• His relationship with his friends also changes. At first, he cares a lot about what his friends think of him, and behaves cruelly in order to impress them. For example when trying to force Sinbad to drink lighter fluid he thinks "this was terrible; in front of the others, I couldn't sort out my little brother". Here, Paddy worries more about not having the power to control his brother than how dangerous drinking lighter fluid would be. This shows that he wants to seem powerful in front of other people and belong to the group, as all his friends commit violent acts during the novel. Later on, Paddy realises that belonging to the group does not protect him and he can't rely on his friends - when he is attacked by Charley Leavy, he says "no one had jumped in for me". He becomes more independent and learns to look after himself.

• The most dramatic shift comes at the end when his father leaves home. Paddy shows that he is mature by describing himself as "the man of the house now". He is no longer dependent upon his father and friends, instead he has started to become someone who other people depend on.

(Remember, there are 4 marks available for correct spelling, punctuation and grammar.)

English Literature Paper 2 — Section A

When you're writing answers for your poetry exam, make sure you really focus on the language the poet chooses, especially the images used and why they are so effective. When you're writing about language, use plenty of quotations from the poem to back up your opinions with examples. Here are some good points you could make for Literature Paper 2:

1) • 'Singh Song!' and 'Les Grands Seigneurs' are both written in the first person, as if the narrator is speaking directly to the reader. 'Les Grands Seigneurs' is narrated by a single voice, which makes the narrator seem isolated and alone. In contrast, 'Singh Song!' features the voices of the narrator, his wife and his customers, which gives the impression that he is part of a larger community of people.

• At first, the narrator of 'Les Grands Seigneurs' sounds romantic and old-fashioned, for example when she says "We played at courtly love". This makes her sound like she enjoyed playing the part of the "damsel" even though it wasn't real. Her language becomes more realistic and modern in the final stanza, when she says she was "a bit of fluff". This makes her sounds bitter and sad about her current relationship.

• In 'Singh Song!' the narrator sounds more light-hearted. The narrator uses a mixture of English and Indian words and accents which are written in phonetic language, such as "he vunt me not to hav a break". This shows that both cultures are important to the narrator, and the use of phonetic language shows that a person's voice is an important part of their identity. He also invents words like "brightey", which suggests that he likes to play with the English language.

• Whereas the voice in 'Les Grands Seigneurs' sounds quite slow and sad, like someone remembering the past, 'Singh Song!' is much more upbeat and happy. Rhymes such as "chutney" and "Putney" and the repetition of the chorus "Hey Singh, ver yoo bin?" makes it sounds like a song.

2) • 'A Vision' describes plans for a future town. At first it sounds like a positive and "beautiful place". The "smoked glass and tubular steel" in the model make the place sound exciting and modern.

• However, the narrator then uses words like "board game suburbs" and "fuzzy-felt grass" to describe the plans for the town. This sounds as if the poet thinks the architects' plans are silly and childish, as if such a place could not exist.

• The poem ends in the present, which is shown to be a very different place to the "dreams" of the future. The narrator is standing at a "landfill site" when he pulls "that future out of the north wind". This image shows that the hopeful plans for the future have been thrown away. It shows that the present is a disappointing place, and contrasts with people's hopes at the beginning.

• The poem 'London' also presents a negative attitude towards a place. The poet uses lots of images of pain and disease to show that it is not a nice place to live. The people have "marks of weakness" and the city is infected "with plagues". There is no hope for a better future as there once was in 'A Vision'.

• The narrator of 'London' also sounds angry at people in charge of the city. He describes the "blood down palace-walls". This image suggests the rich hide behind their walls and do nothing to stop the suffering. This presents the place as unequal and unfair. It also contrasts with the childlike images of "fuzzy-felt grass" in 'A Vision'.

3)
- 'The Right Word' is about a conflict which has led to suspicious attitudes towards other people, and 'Flag' is about conflict caused by loyalty to your country.
- 'The Right Word' uses repeated images to present the conflict. Repetition of the phrase "outside the door" shows that there is a barrier separating the speaker and the stranger. By repeating "in the shadows" the poem suggests that the stranger can't be seen clearly, which is why the narrator doesn't trust him.
- The images in 'Flag' are vivid and painful, such as "the guts of men" and "the blood you bleed". These images present conflict as dangerous and violent.
- The narrator of 'The Right Word' uses words such as "terrorist" and "hostile militant" to describe a stranger. These words show that she feels scared of him. It suggests that a conflict has led her to be suspicious of people so she suspects all strangers are dangerous.
- 'The Right Word' ends on a positive message. The narrator realises that he "is a child who looks like mine" and invites him in. This shows that an attitude of trust can solve the effects of conflict.
- 'Flag' has an angrier message. It mocks the fact that a flag can have so much power over people. It says that people who fight over a flag must "blind your conscience". This suggests that people who fight for their country are ignoring their own morals.

4)
- The narrator of 'Nettles' feels protective of his son and when he falls in nettles he "soothed him". The image of "white blisters" on his "tender skin" is a painful contrast. These vivid images show how upset the narrator was by his innocent son's pain.
- His anger towards the nettles show how strongly he cares for his son. He "slashed in fury", as if he was desperate to get rid of possible danger. Also, he describes the nettles as a "regiment of spite", which makes them sound like an evil army.
- However, his protective feelings for his son are complicated. He wants to always protect him, but knows that he "would often feel sharp wounds again". It shows that he is aware that he is helpless to stop his son getting hurt.
- The narrator of 'Born Yesterday' also feels protective towards a child, but his feelings are shown in his hopes for her future rather than his actions.
- His hopes are unusual because he wants her to be ordinary — "not ugly, not good-looking". This suggests that his feelings for her are more practical.

- It seems as if he is making fun of other wishes for her, such as the traditional "innocence and love". This shows that his hopes for her are more helpful, because they are realistic. In this way, he is like the narrator of 'Nettles' who is realistic about being unable to completely protect his son.

5)
- 'Kid' is entertaining because it puts two well-known characters into new roles, so you see them both differently. For example, it is surprising to see Batman in a "caper with the married woman", because that's very different to the well-known heroic idea of Batman. Also, Robin's old costume of "green and scarlet" is very different to his new, ordinary "jeans and crew-neck jumper". This surprising element is unexpected so it is entertaining.
- The language often sounds as if it is taken straight from a comic book. Phrases like "holy robin-redbreast-nest-egg-shocker!" remind the reader of language used in the comic, which makes the poem sound playful and entertaining.
- The rhyme also adds energy. 'Kid' rhymes all the way through because each line ends on an '-er' sound. This makes the poem sound playful, so it is entertaining and fun to read.
- 'Kid' uses a lot of alliteration like "Batman, big shot" and "punching the palm". The repetition of these sounds make Robin sound angry and loud. This means it is easy to understand Robin's feelings, so the ideas of revenge are more entertaining for the reader.

6)
- 'Cold Knap Lake' is written in the first person so it sounds personal, as if the narrator is telling us about an event from her past.
- The memories in 'Cold Knap Lake' sound very clear and definite to begin with. The descriptions are detailed — she remembers that the child was "blue-lipped" and covered in the "long green silk" of weeds. The colours and images are vivid, so the reader believes the narrator remembers it well.
- The descriptions of the characters' actions make the event seem real and dramatic. For example, the image of her mother giving "a stranger's child her breath" whilst being watched by a "silent" crowd brings the scene to life by describing the different actions and senses.
- The mood of the poem changes in the last two stanzas. The short, direct question of "was I there?" tells the reader that the narrator doesn't actually remember the event well. She is suddenly uncertain, so the reader doesn't know whether to believe her or trust her description of the event.

• The last two stanzas show the true nature of memories more than the clear, confident descriptions at the beginning. Childhood memories are often confusing and forgotten, and the image of a "shadowy" and "troubled surface" bring this to life very well.

7) • The images in 'Being Boring' are simple, everyday images that highlight how ordinary and plain the narrator's life is. She tells us that she had "a slight cold" which is an uninteresting detail. She describes herself as a "happier cabbage" which links her to vegetables and gardening, which could be seen as quite mundane.

• There is repetition of the phrase "I want to go on being boring". This highlights the message of the poem, but it also shows that her life is full of repetition.

• The rhyme and rhythm are both regular, so the poem sounds steady and predictable. This reflects the ordinary, unexciting description of her life.

• The narrator's tone is bold. She refuses to answer a question because "I have nothing to say", and challenges the reader with direct questions such as "what are they for?". Everyone is accusing her of being boring but she is arguing that she is happy with her life.

• However, her defence of a boring life is not always believable. When she is arguing that she just wants to stay at home with her partner, the image of him "eating and sleeping and snoring" makes him sound unattractive. She says "I get on with my work. He gets on with his", which suggests their relationship is not loving or exciting.

• The narrator sounds unfriendly when she says parties are pointless unless you "need to find a new lover". It sounds as if she is only interested in having a boyfriend and has no other hobbies or ambitions.

8) • I found this poem surprising because the act of stealing a snowman is "unusual". The narrator's attitude towards this act is also shocking and uncaring — they say they found it exciting "knowing that children will cry in the morning". This casual attitude towards stealing continues through the poem. For example words like "pinch" and "nicked" make the narrator sound chatty and relaxed, so it seems as if they don't care.

• The narrator also has a surprising attitude towards the snowman. He's described as "magnificent", showing that the narrator admires the snowman. The narrator also wants him as "a mate", which

suggests that they feel closer to the snowman than the people they're stealing from. It seems shocking that someone can be so isolated from other people.

• The narrator's actions are surprising, for example they "booted" the snowman and destroyed it, even though they wanted it and it "took some time" to re-build. This pointless act highlights how frustrated the narrator feels.

• The image of being "so bored I could eat myself" is very dramatic. It's shocking because it shows that they are angry at their own life as well as everyone else, and have self-destructive thoughts.

• The end is a surprising change of tone — the narrator speaks to the reader in a direct question. Saying "you don't understand a word I'm saying, do you?" shows that the narrator feels disconnected.

9) • I think the most striking thing about Heaney's memories of his father is how much he respects him. He uses language that makes the digging sound skilful and tough, such as "nestled on the lug" and "levered firmly".

• It is also striking how clear his memories are. The poem is full of images and Heaney uses many senses to describe the scene, so it really comes alive. He describes the sounds of "nicking and slicing", the feel of "cool hardness", and the smell of "potato mould".

• The sound of the words used is very important. The alliteration of "tall tops" and "buried the bright" gives the poem the rhythm of someone digging. The noise of the words "squelch and slap" mimics the noises the spade makes in the mud.

• Halfway through, an exclamation of "By God, the old man could handle a spade" breaks through the detailed descriptions. The difference in tone makes the statement sound honest, as if the narrator is talking directly to us.

• When the narrator says "I've no spade" it shows how different he feels from his father. The narrator just has a pen between his "finger and thumb" whilst his father does physical work. These images suggest the narrator feels inferior to his father. But then he says "I'll dig" with his pen, which links writing and digging. This suggests Heaney still feels linked to the memory of his father, despite their differences.

10) • 'Having a Word' gives a negative impression of society. The poet is saying that big ideas about "equality" and "liberation" are not enough to make a difference to people's lives.

• The first stanza challenges you to think about big ideas because it uses words that you think are very similar but then says the ideas behind them are not the same at all. For example, "freedom may not mean liberation". This makes the reader think about what freedom and liberation really mean.

• The narrator examines what words mean to unsettle the reader and to show that our society is not as safe as we might think. The line "Intelligence may not mean intelligent" suggests we shouldn't just accept the government's rules as they might not know best.

• However, the narrator is quite positive about individuals. He addresses the reader as "my friend" and "dear neighbour", which creates a connection and suggests that the reader can trust him. He also says "you are greater than the law" which suggests that individuals have the power to change their society for the better.

• The final line — "to be awake may not mean to be conscious" — uses word-play to challenge ideas, but is more personal. Instead of criticising society as a whole, this makes the reader think about their own role within that society.

English Literature Paper 2 — Section B

11) • This poem is narrated by a man watching his daughter run into the sea, as he follows behind. The tone is personal because the narrator uses the word "you". This shows he's talking to his daughter about his feelings for her.

• The images show the differences between father and daughter. She "ran" into the sea but he "ploughed", she throws off clothes "like the seasons" which he "caught in my arms". These show that she is young and carefree, whereas he has more responsibility.

• He describes himself as the "guardian" of her "little heart" which makes him sound protective of his young daughter. However, then we're told that she was "not quite thirteen" and brave enough to go "swimming in the Atlantic". He can't help thinking of her as a little girl, even though she's growing up.

• The image of him with his hands "full of / all the years" could have many meanings. It could mean he feels old compared to his daughter and wishes he could throw off "the city's years". But it could also represent years of memories of his daughter's childhood, which he wants to keep safe.

• I think the most important idea in the poem is that the father "knew he could not follow" and stays behind watching her. The whole poem is about him letting his daughter go because she is growing up, even though it makes him sad.

12) • Both poems are set at the beach, and show characters running or jumping into the sea. They both use energetic images to show the freedom this brings, such as "then let fly" in 'Pier', or "throwing off shoes" in 'Donegal'. These images remind the reader of their own seaside holidays.

• Both poems use the word "you" to show they are speaking to someone directly. This makes both poems feel very personal, as it sounds like they're talking directly to the reader.

• Both poems follow a similar structure. They start on the beach and then move towards the sea, which gives each poem a sense of suspense as the reader wonders when the characters will enter the water, or what will happen when they do.

• In contrast with 'Donegal', 'Pier' focuses more on the physical actions of jumping into the sea. The description is very detailed, for example — "slit water, drag it open, catch your breath". This means it's very easy for the reader to imagine the scene. On the other hand, the descriptions in 'Donegal' focus on the feelings instead of the actions. The action of "throwing off shoes" is compared to throwing off "the city's years". This description reminds the reader of the freedom of running into the sea.

• 'Donegal' is written using the past tense. This makes it sound more thoughtful, as the narrator is looking back on the event and remembering his feelings. 'Pier' uses the present tense, so it sounds as if it's actually happening right now.

• The endings are very different. 'Donegal' ends quite sadly, with the father remembering that he "could not follow" his daughter. 'Pier' ends happily, because the narrator says you can "Do it over" which suggests that this happiness and freedom is possible for anyone.

English Literature Paper 3 — Section A

1) a) *For this question, pay close attention to the language used by both characters and what it shows about them and their relationship. You need to think about what the audience would think of them because of how they act here.*
Here are a few good points you could include:

• The extract is a comic scene between Benedick and Beatrice which presents the characters as witty and likeable, despite their insulting conversation. Although this is the first time that the audience sees the two characters meet in the play, there are hints that they already know each other and had a close relationship in the past, for example, Beatrice says, "I know you of old". This increases the tension of the scene as the audience is unsure whether their insults are playful or serious.

• Beatrice and Benedick are presented as unafraid of insulting the other person's appearance and character. Benedick calls Beatrice "Lady Disdain!" while Beatrice says that scratching Benedick's face "could not make it worse". Both characters seem strong and feisty, particularly Beatrice who does not conform to the traditional stereotype of women at the time as quiet and shy.

• Both characters use quick wordplay which shows they are witty and intelligent. They both use similar imagery, for example animal imagery such as "parrot-teacher", "beast" and "jade's trick". This shows that they are equally matched in intelligence and able to play off each other's insults, as if they can guess what the next person is about to say.

• Both characters agree that they are not interested in love or marriage. Benedick says, "truly, I love none" and Beatrice says "I had rather hear my dog bark at a crow than a man swear he loves me." Although both Beatrice and Benedick reject love, they seem perfectly matched and this suggests to the audience that they may change their mind about love.

b) *In this question, you need to write about the play as a whole, picking out the important bits which tell the audience something about the relationship between Hero and Claudio. Here are a few good points you could include in your answer:*

• Claudio first talks about his love for Hero when he speaks to Benedick in Act 1 Scene 1. He says "I love her, I feel" and describes her as the "sweetest lady" and a "jewel". Claudio has loving feelings towards Hero, even though he has not spoken to her yet. This suggests that his love for Hero is based on her beauty and her family's wealth rather than her personality.

• Hero and Claudio get engaged quickly, with Don Pedro wooing Hero for Claudio. Hero is silent when the lovers meet, only whispering in Claudio's ear that "he is in her heart". Hero's silence shows that she is playing the traditional role of the young, shy virgin. From this point, Claudio becomes a typical courtly lover, showering Hero with gifts and poems.

• When Hero is accused of being unfaithful, Claudio accepts Don John's proof immediately, instead of trusting Hero. Despite his previous love for her, he cannot get past his belief that she "knows the heat of a luxurious bed". Claudio rejects Hero because he believes that her virginity, an important thing in Elizabethan society, has been ruined. His quick rejection of Hero shows that his love for her is shallow.

• When Hero reveals herself to be Claudio's bride at the end of the play, Claudio declares that she is "Another Hero!" and Hero says that in the past Claudio was "my other husband". This suggests that their relationship has been strengthened by the difficulties they have overcome, since now they are like different people.

2) a) *For this question you need to work out not just what Lady Macbeth is thinking and feeling, but also how Shakespeare is getting those thoughts and feelings across. Here are some things you could say:*

• Lady Macbeth makes this speech when she's waiting for Duncan to arrive at her castle, and she's thinking about how to kill the king.

• Lady Macbeth is trying to get rid of all the things that make her a women, like "breasts" and "milk", calling on the spirits to "unsex me here". She wants to lose the qualities that women were traditionally expected to have and become more masculine and violent.

• She is calling on supernatural powers, "Come, you Spirits / That tend on mortal thoughts", to do something unnatural. In Macbeth, with its witches, calling on evil spirits seems likely to have an effect. The alliteration in "sightless substances" also makes her speech seem like a spell.

• Shakespeare fills her speech with words associated with the human body like "blood" and "gall". These physical images are made unnatural too as she says "Make thick my blood". This links her speech back to the murder as that is an unnatural, bloody attack on a body.

• When she says she wants to be filled up with cruelty, she says from "crown to the toe". While crown means head here, it could also suggest she's thinking about the aim of her cruelty — becoming queen.

b) *For these kinds of questions you'll want to pick a bit that you've studied well. Make sure you get points in about both thoughts and feelings — and remember to look at the techniques Shakespeare used to create them.*

For example, Lady Macbeth in Act V, Scene I

• In this scene, a doctor and a gentlewoman watch Lady Macbeth walking and talking in her sleep. The fact that she is so worried even in her sleep suggests that she is struggling to cope with what she has done.

• Shakespeare has Lady Macbeth speaking in prose here. This contrasts with the way she speaks in verse earlier in the play. This suggests that she's lost control of her thoughts and speech.

• Lady Macbeth in this scene is trying desperately to wash off the blood she imagines is on her hands. The fact she is obsessed with blood is a sign that guilt has driven her to madness: "… who would have thought the old man to have had so much blood in him?". The physical action of Lady Macbeth frantically trying to rub the blood from her hands emphasises the madness of her speech to the audience watching the play.

• Shakespeare makes it seem as if the guilt is too much for Lady Macbeth to bear when she speaks in nonsense, child-like rhymes: "The Thane of Fife had a wife". Her life has become more than she can handle and she is going mad.

• Shakespeare shows that the terrible murders are weighing on her mind as she gives up her secrets so easily: "I tell you yet again, Banquo's buried; he cannot come out on's grave." The doctor says that people with "infected minds" often need to "discharge their secrets" even if it's when they're sleeping, which shows that Lady Macbeth feels she has something to confess.

3) a) *For this question you'll need to look carefully at the language used in this extract, but keep in mind where it fits into the play. And don't forget what you've learnt about the characters involved. Here are some things you could say:*

• Mercutio has just been stabbed by Tybalt in a fight, and he is about to die. Shakespeare makes this dramatic at first as Mercutio, usually a funny character, continues to joke even as he's dying. This makes Romeo and the audience believe that he might survive, which creates suspense.

• Mercutio can't help making jokes even as he's dying. Though his plays on words are interesting and amusing, they are also quite grim. He says his wound is not "so wide as a church door" and tells them that tomorrow he will be a "grave man".

• Even as Mercutio is joking with his friend Romeo, he is angry with him. It's Romeo's quarrel with Tybalt which has cost him his life. Mercutio isn't a Montague or a Capulet, and he's angry that he's been killed for a fight that wasn't his. His line "A plague o'both your houses" is dramatic because it sounds so angry and full of hate, and contrasts with his usual jokes. It almost sounds like a curse on the Montagues and the Capulets, given Romeo and Juliet's deaths later.

• Mercutio's anger at Tybalt is dramatic and he continues to mock him even as he dies: "Zounds, a dog, a rat, a mouse, a cat, to scratch a man to death". This makes Mercutio seem almost surprised that it should be Tybalt who kills him, and in keeping with his character, he continues to taunt him.

b) *For this question you'll want to pick a scene from the play that you've studied carefully and know well. Pick one of the really dramatic scenes where something big is happening — it'll make things a lot easier.*

For example, for Act V, Scene III

• The start of this scene is dramatic as Paris and Romeo meet accidentally. What makes it so dramatic is that we know that Juliet isn't dead but neither Paris nor Romeo do.

• Shakespeare's language makes it clear that Romeo is upset and out of control. Romeo compares his aims to "empty tigers or the roaring sea", which makes him seem like a force of nature that can't be stopped or controlled. This creates tension, as the audience wants to find out what he will do.

• Paris fights Romeo because he thinks he's going into the tomb to do "villainous shame / To the dead bodies". Paris doesn't know Romeo and Juliet are married. This is ironic as once again in the play the characters don't know the facts of the situation, while the audience do, so this creates suspense and drama.

• Shakespeare makes Paris seem like an honest and innocent person here, grieving for Juliet "with tears distill'd by moans." This makes it even more sad when he is killed by Romeo, because we don't feel that he has done anything wrong.

• When Romeo enters the tomb, Shakespeare makes it more dramatic by focusing on the details that show that Juliet isn't dead. Romeo says that she still looks beautiful and has colour in her cheeks: "Beauty's ensign yet / Is crimson on thy lips and in thy cheeks". This is ironic — these signs of life are there because she is still alive, as the audience knows, which increases the drama of the scene.

English Literature Paper 3 —Section B

4) a) *For this part of the question, you need to look at the character of Napoleon and how he changes throughout the novel. The question also asks you about the society presented, which means you should discuss how Napoleon's behaviour affects the whole of Animal Farm, and link that to relevant events in Soviet Russia. Here are some points you could make:*

• At the beginning of the novel, Napoleon is a common pig, equal to the rest of the animals. However, we're told in chapter 2 that he has a "reputation for getting his own way". Early in the story, Napoleon is shown to be selfish because he doesn't mind sacrificing other animals to get what he wants. For example, he doesn't take part in the Battle of the Cowshed, but benefits from the farm being saved.

• He later claims to have been the hero who was responsible for the victory, and rewrites history so that Snowball was working with Jones. This shows how Napoleon has complete control, not only over what the other animals do, but also what they believe. 'Animal Farm' is an allegory which shows many parallels between the story and events in Soviet Russia. Like Napoleon, Stalin rewrote history to make his own part in the Russian revolution seem more important as he rose to power.

• As Napoleon becomes more powerful, the reader realises that he is also dishonest and cruel. This is shown when he lies about educating the dogs so he could use violence to steal power from Snowball. The dogs are like Stalin's secret police in the Soviet Union — both the dogs and the secret police used force to make sure that the citizens were scared and obedient. Throughout the book Napoleon twists the truth to get what he wants. For example, he called the windmill "nonsense" but then claimed it was "his creation". This part of the novel is a parallel to Stalin seizing power from Trotsky through a combination of rumour-spreading and violence, finally driving Trotsky from the Soviet Union.

• Napoleon's cruelty and lying get much worse as his power increases. He uses Squealer to spread lies about "Snowball's treachery" and forces many animals to admit they betrayed Napoleon under Snowball's orders. Napoleon then kills the animals who confess "until there was a pile of corpses lying before Napoleon's feet". This dramatic scene mirrors the executions that were common when Stalin ruled Russia. Stalin was a dictator, and Orwell presents Napoleon as a cruel, selfish dictator in 'Animal Farm'.

b) *For this part of the question, focus on how Napoleon behaves towards the other animals, and how his increasing power changes this. You get marks for showing understanding of the context, so explain how certain events in the novel link to Soviet Russia. Here are some points you could make:*

• Napoleon is first introduced as "not much of a talker", and it seems the "vivacious" Snowball is more popular with the other animals. Napoleon's early relationship with the other animals is based on lies and secrets. For example, he distracts them from the milk by saying "the harvest is more important" and then steals the milk for the pigs. This is similar to events in the Soviet Union, when grain shortages prompted Stalin to seize grain supplies from farmers, which led to famine. Napoleon is always scheming to get what he wants, and to make sure the pigs live very comfortably.

• Napoleon gradually surrounds himself with ceremonies and followers to make him seem more important. He is always followed by the pack of dogs, and eventually a black cockerel who acts like "a kind of trumpeter". He starts being called "our Leader, Comrade Napoleon" and also "awarded himself 'animal hero, first class' ". These signs of power hide his weaknesses from the other animals, so they admire him.

• Napoleon also becomes more controlling of the other animals. The meetings and debates are cancelled, so the other animals have no control over farm decisions. The commandments are gradually changed, but his dogs growl "threateningly" when someone questions this, which links to the threats made by Stalin's police force.

• Squealer is important because he spreads propaganda about Napoleon, and speaks "so persuasively" that he convinces the animals of Napoleon's greatness. This shows how Napoleon uses Squealer to present himself in a positive light, just as Stalin used propaganda. Through Squealer's lies, Napoleon can control the animals without even speaking to them himself.

• Eventually, most of the animals believe in the fake image of a wise and wonderful leader, and agree with Boxer's motto that "Napoleon is always right". The animals not fooled by Squealer's lies are too afraid of Napoleon's violence to argue. In the end, he has complete control over them.

5) a) *For this part of the question, you don't need to write down absolutely everything that happens, you just need to describe the most important events.*

• Utterson writes a letter to Jekyll complaining about having been barred from his house and asking for the cause of Jekyll's argument with Dr Lanyon.

• He receives an answer the next day from Jekyll, which says that he is going to live "a life of extreme seclusion." He says this has come about because, as he says, "I have brought on myself a punishment and a danger that I cannot name."

• Dr Lanyon dies, and it's suggested that part of the cause of his death is his discovery of the horrifying truth about Dr Jekyll.

• Utterson opens the letter from the now dead Dr Lanyon, which contains another letter which is only to be opened on the death or disappearance of Dr Jekyll.

• Utterson continues to call on Jekyll, "but he was perhaps relieved to be denied admittance." Jekyll keeps himself locked away on his own in the cabinet above the laboratory.

b) *This question is asking about the writer's techniques, which includes things like style and language. Give examples of horrifying parts of the extract and explain how language is used to make them so shocking for the reader.*

• There's a big contrast in Jekyll's attitude before and after he senses the change coming over him: "… the words were hardly uttered, before the smile was struck out of his face…" This sudden dramatic change in attitude surprises the reader and makes the extract shocking.

• Utterson speaks to Jekyll "good-naturedly" and when the doctor responds, his tone is both friendly and formal; "That is just what I was about to venture to propose". This is very different to the sudden shocked silence that takes place moments later. This contrast adds to the shock and horror of the extract.

• Stevenson makes the extract shocking and horrifying by focusing on the reaction of Utterson and Enfield. They aren't sick or troubled in the way that Jekyll is, so their reactions make us feel that the look on Jekyll's face was something truly terrible. We are told that Jekyll's sudden expression of terror "froze the very blood of the two gentlemen below." The incident has a physical impact on Utterson and Enfield; they stay silent for some time and they are described as "both pale", with an "answering horror in their eyes", which shows how shocked they were.

• The description of Jekyll at the beginning of this extract helps to make his sudden change of attitude more horrifying. He is described as "taking the air with an infinite sadness of mien, like some disconsolate prisoner." This suggests that he is both made miserable and trapped by what is affecting him.

• Stevenson makes the incident more shocking by making it happen so fast. Utterson and Enfield only see the look of terror on Jekyll's face "but for a glimpse". It is so horrifying that even that glimpse is enough to terrify them.

c) *This question focuses on how the author presents the character of Utterson. You only need to talk about the descriptions of Utterson in this extract, so don't write about the way he behaves in other parts of the novel.*

• When Utterson sees Jekyll at the window looking miserable, he suggests the solution to Jekyll's sickness: "You stay too much indoors… You should be out, whipping up the circulation like Mr Enfield and me." This makes him seem like someone with a straightforward and commonsense view of things, in contrast to the more mysterious and complicated Dr Jekyll.

• That he clearly cares for his friend is shown by the way he tries to put Dr Jekyll at ease. When Jekyll says that he can neither come down, nor let them up to speak to him, Utterson replies that "the best thing we can do is stay down here and speak with you from where we are." This makes it seem that he's quite willing to do things to help his friend. He's also described as speaking "good-naturedly", which makes him seem like a decent person.

• Utterson's shock at the look on his friend's face could show how much he cares for Jekyll. It suggests that Utterson is someone whose old friends are important to him and who cares about people.

d) *This final part of the question is your chance to show that you know the rest of the novel well. The key thing here is to pick another part of the book that you're familiar with - that way you'll already have lots to say and you can be confident when you answer the question.*

For example, for the chapter 'Dr. Jekyll was Quite at Ease.'

• Dr Jekyll seems in control of himself here. When Utterson mentions the will: "A close observer might have gathered that the topic was distasteful; but the doctor carried it off gaily." This shows that he doesn't want to talk about it, but he behaves as if it's not a big problem.

• He attacks Lanyon, and says "I was never more disappointed in any man than Lanyon." This makes it seem that Jekyll hasn't fully realised the terrible mistake he's made. This attack on an old friend also suggests that there is a dark side to his character, and that this dark side might be getting stronger.

• Jekyll also reveals his temper in the way he acts in this extract. After trying to hide his distaste for talking about the will, he responds to Utterson saying that he doesn't approve of it "a trifle sharply". This suggests that Jekyll is trying to repress his anger, and that Utterson has touched a nerve.

• As the discussion progresses, Dr Jekyll is described as acting with an "incoherency of manner". This suggests that maintaining a double life is tricky, and it is taking its toll on the doctor.

• Dr Jekyll misleads Utterson here about the true nature of his relationship with Hyde. As he asks Utterson to make sure that Hyde is given his inheritance, he lays "his hand upon the other's arm". This shows that they are old friends, but also that he's taking advantage of their friendship.

6) *This question wants you to think carefully about the language Golding has used to set the scene. You need to consider not only the actual description of the island but how the characters see the island too. Remember you're only analysing the extract in the question, so if you mention the language used to describe the island in other parts of the book you'll just be wasting time.*

• Everything on the island seems to be either pink or green, and Golding describes it as having "peacock water". These bright colours make the reader imagine the island as a tropical paradise and make it seem beautiful, exotic and safe.

• The island also seems unreal, as if it belongs in a book or a fairy story. The coral looks like it has been "scribbled" by a giant, and the boys recognise the coral because they've "seen pictures like that". In this extract, Golding describes the island like the ones in the adventure stories such as 'Coral Island' that he goes on to challenge.

• Even though we know it's not, the island feels as if it might be man-made. It's "boat-shaped" and there are references to other man-made things like "an aquarium". The island has been damaged in places, but this is also the fault of humans, because Jack says that the "gash visible in the trees" is "where we landed".

• The boys feel that they know what the island is like because in this extract they are high up, so they have a good view of everything. They can see "a circular horizon of water" all the way round the island, and their view is "not robbed of sharpness by mirage". The island seems safe because they can see everything clearly and there's nothing to threaten them.

• The boys also feel that they have power over the island because they are "triumphant". This is probably because their surroundings seem familiar to them — the separate rock, "standing like a fort", might give them the sense that the island is their Empire.

• Although the island looks like a place of paradise on the outside, on the inside the boys have turned the island into a living hell. This emphasises Golding's idea that humans all have evil within, and has some similarities to the story of the Garden of Eden.

7) *This question wants you to give your opinion on Ralph at the end of the story. You can't go too far wrong as long as you make sure you use quotes to back up anything you say.*

• At the end of the novel, we feel sorry for Ralph because we see him through the officer's eyes as "a kid" who needs "a bath, a hair-cut, a nose-wipe and a good deal of ointment". His needs make him seem young and vulnerable, as if he needs looking after.

• We feel sorry for him because he seems to have lost the ability to express himself clearly. He answers the officer "shyly" and can't seem to finish sentences: "We were together then –". This is very different from the way he was at the start of the novel, when he "found he could talk fluently and explain what he had to say".

• However, we also admire Ralph, because he admits that he's the "boss", even though the officer criticises them for not putting up "a better show than that." This contrasts with the behaviour of Jack who "started forward, then changed his mind and stood still." It's also the one moment during the ending where Ralph speaks clearly — when the officer asks who's in charge, Ralph answers "loudly".

• At the end of the novel Ralph suddenly seems to understand things. He is aware of "the end of innocence" and "the darkness of man's heart." This makes us feel impressed that he has such a mature understanding of what has happened, but sad because it shows us that his childhood has come to a sudden end.

Index

Index

Index

Acknowledgements

The publisher would like to thank the following copyright holders for permission to reproduce texts and images:

Page 18:   Fireworks and Animals leaflet © The Blue Cross, www.bluecross.org.uk

Page 19:   Article entitled, 'British teenager becomes youngest person to sail round the world solo' by Caroline Davies, copyright Guardian News & Media Ltd 2009.
With thanks to Rex Features for permission to reproduce the photograph

Page 20:   'When Danger Starts at Home' article, with thanks to Habitat for Humanity for permission to use the webpage

Page 123:   Photo and article entitled, 'Record Dragons' Den investment for Harry Potter-style magic wand' © Telegraph Media Group Limited 2010

Page 124:   Article entitled 'Jamie Oliver' © Hello! Magazine.com
With thanks to Rex Features for permission to reproduce the photograph

Page 125:   Article reproduced with permission of Lonely Planet. © 2006 Lonely Planet

Page 128:   Extract from *Hobson's Choice* by Harold Brighouse, reproduced by permission of the publisher & author representatives, Samuel French

Page 132:   Extract from *Of Mice and Men by John Steinbeck (Penguin, 2000). Copyright © John Steinbeck, 1937, 1965. Reproduced by permission of Penguin Books Ltd.*

Page 134:   Extract from *Paddy Clarke Ha! Ha! Ha!* By Roddy Doyle, published by Secker & Warburg. Reprinted by permission of The Random House Group Ltd

Page 138:   'Pier' by Vona Groarke, reproduced by kind permission of the author and The Gallery Press, Loughcrew, Oldcastle, County Meath, Ireland from *Spindrift* (2009)

'Donegal' by Robin Robertson, reproduced by permission of Pan Macmillan Copyright © Robin Robertson, 2006

Make sure you're not missing out on another superb CGP revision book that might just save your life...

...order your **free** catalogue today.

EFS41